EYES OF THE WORLD

EYES OF THE

MARC ARONSON & MARINA BUDHOS

WORLD

ROBERT CAPA, GERDA TARO,
AND THE INVENTION OF
MODERN PHOTOJOURNALISM

HENRY HOLT AND COMPANY | NEW YORK

Henry Holt and Company, *Publishers since 1866*
175 Fifth Avenue, New York, New York 10010
fiercereads.com

Library of Congress Cataloging-in-Publication Data
Names: Aronson, Marc, author. | Budhos, Marina Tamar, author.
Title: Eyes of the world : Robert Capa, Gerda Taro, and the invention of
modern photojournalism / Marc Aronson and Marina Budhos.
Description: New York : Henry Holt and Company, [2017]
Includes bibliographical references and index.
Identifiers: LCCN 2016020545 (print) | LCCN 2016033064 (ebook)
ISBN 9780805098358 (hardcover) | ISBN 9781250109675 (ebook)
Subjects: LCSH: Photojournalists—Europe—Biography. | Capa, Robert, 1913–1954. | Taro, Gerda,
1910–1937. | Spain—History—Civil War, 1936–1939—Biography. | Spain—History—Civil War,
1936–1939—Photography. | Photojournalism. | War photographers—Europe—Biography.
Classification: LCC TR139 .A76 2017 (print) | LCC TR139 (ebook) | DDC 770—dc23
LC record available at https://lccn.loc.gov/2016020545

Our books may be purchased in bulk for promotional, educational, or business use.
Please contact your local bookseller or the Macmillan Corporate and Premium Sales Department at
(800) 221-7945 ext. 5442 or by e-mail at MacmillanSpecialMarkets@macmillan.com.

First Edition—2017 / Designed by April Ward
Printed in China

1   3   5   7   9   10   8   6   4   2

To the memory of Lisa Jalowetz Aronson,
who knew all about love, life, and artistic collaboration

NOTE TO THE READER

For further details on where, when, and by whom each photo was taken, please see icp.org/browse/archive/collections/eyes-of-the-world, kindly created for us by the International Center for Photography. Attributions used there and in this book rely on the most recent scholarship and are more authoritative than older books and Web sites.

You will find maps related to the events in this book on pages ix, 45, 121, and 203. For additional information on the people, political parties, and events in this book, please use the resources beginning on page 250. You will find:

- A full cast of characters with mini biographies of individual artists, journalists, memoirists, novelists, photographers, poets, and politicians.

- A breakdown of the competing political parties in Spain.

- An outline of forces and individuals from outside of Spain who played a part in its civil war.

- A detailed time line of the events treated here with relevant world context.

CONTENTS

EUROPE
1936

ESTONIA

SOVIET UNION

DENMARK

IRISH
FREE
STATE

LATVIA

LITHUANIA

ENGLAND

NETHERLANDS

BELGIUM

GERMANY

POLAND

LUXEMBOURG

CZECHOSLOVAKIA

FRANCE

SWITZERLAND

AUSTRIA

HUNGARY

ROMANIA

PORTUGAL

YUGOSLAVIA

SPAIN

ITALY

ALBANIA

BULGARIA

GREECE

TURKEY

SPANISH MOROCCO

American soldiers huddle behind barriers to avoid enemy fire as they approach Omaha Beach early on June 6, 1944—D-Day. The Germans had planted these steel obstacles and linked them to explosive mines to hamper landing craft. To capture the moment, Capa had to be in the water, dodging bullets like the rest of the men.

PROLOGUE

BOB'S STORY

NORMANDY, JUNE 6, 1944

AS ROBERT CAPA TELLS IT: A metal ramp cranks open and lands with a splashing thud. Chilly dawn fog rushes into the craft where thirty soldiers sit shivering, crouched on benches. The floor sways, slick with vomit; the seas have been rough. Ahead, these men know, is a most dangerous mission: they must capture a slender, crescent-shaped strip of beach at the bottom of towering cliffs in Normandy, France. At the top are hundreds of Nazi troops, stationed in their bunkers behind machine guns and mortar pits, waiting.

Capa, the only photographer to land with the initial wave of the mission, removes one of his two cameras from its oilskin cover just as the rush of men clamber into the freezing water, rifles held over their heads. From the bluffs, a rain of machine-gun fire breaks out; within seconds, dozens are falling into the waves. The sea pools red, but there is no stopping the soldiers swarming off similar barges, pushing into the foaming shallows toward Omaha Beach.

Capa follows, repeating to himself words he learned in Spain: *Es una cosa muy seria.* This is a very serious business.

Capa is photographing the first moments of D-Day—the crucial invasion planned by the Allies. For five years, war has raged across Europe. With the attack on Pearl Harbor in 1941, America was drawn in. Capa risks everything to capture the story of World War II, the global fight against fascism. He takes risks all the time—judging; figuring out which missions to go on, which dangers are worth braving, which conflicts magazines will assign him to cover. He has been to Italy during the Allied advance, where he covered nightmarish scenes in Naples.

In the spring of 1944, he stayed in London, where everyone seemed to be aware of an imminent and yet absolutely secret invasion plan. Then, in late May, Capa was summoned to military headquarters on the coast of England, where

Soldiers who made it through the obstacles and strafing fire scrambled to reach the beach and dig in.

The soldier whose face is barely visible in Capa's photo has been identified as Private First Class Huston Riley, who was injured in the invasion but survived.

leaders were planning this most audacious of operations. To enter France from the coast will be crucial to winning the war. Everyone knows this, even the Germans: "We'll have only one chance to stop the enemy, and that's while he's in the water, struggling to get ashore. The first twenty-four hours of the invasion will be decisive," declares German Field Marshal Erwin Rommel.

On the night of June 5, Capa gambles into the wee hours with men who know what awaits them. They are on board the USS *Samuel Chase*, a warship that carries in its belly several barges, each of which will be propelled into the water several hundred feet off the coast of France. Of the two thousand soldiers he accompanies, Capa says, "They are tough experienced men, some have been through invasion before, and now are the spearhead again."

Capa is given a choice. Which unit will he join? Which wave of soldiers, headed directly into the teeth of Nazi guns, should he photograph? He takes one more gamble: he will launch with the boats on the second round of the very first wave—those most at risk. He puts himself as close as possible to the fight.

The landing does not go entirely as planned. The choppy, high waves and current blow many of the boats off course. Now the soldiers, scrambling through the bloodstained waters to shore, find themselves in a different position than was anticipated. Due to overcast weather, B-26 bombers, meant to pound the German positions and create craters where the men can huddle for protection, are dropping their bombs too far inland. Rockets intended to stun the German troops have gone off too soon. The men are advancing on the open beach, where they will be picked off by the German gunners up on the bluffs. Scores of soldiers press themselves into the wet sand, huddling behind the forbidding obstacles the Germans have erected: stakes of metal and concrete and mine-tipped logs that jut up from the shallows.

Crouching behind a steel barrier in the freezing water, Capa keeps photographing. "Exhausted from the water and the fear, we lay flat on a small strip of wet sand between the sea and the barbed wire. The slant of the beach gave us some protection, so long as we lay flat, from the machine-gun and rifle bullets, but the tide pushed us against the barbed wire, where the guns were enjoying open season."

Crawling toward a lieutenant he played poker with the night before, Capa pulls out his second camera, raises his arms, and snaps away while keeping his head bowed down, mortars exploding around him, until he has finished a few film rolls. Then terror seizes hold. "The empty camera trembled in my hands. It was a new kind of fear shaking my body from toe to hair, and twisting my face."

Finally, Capa wades back through the water and climbs onto a landing craft, where he goes up to the deck and shoots his last images of the "smoke covered beach" and the wounded. Then he is back on the *Chase*, helping lift stretchers and photographing the dead and wounded. The next thing he knows, everything goes black.

Capa is covered in a rough blanket with a note that reads, "Exhaustion case. No dog tags."

LANDING WITH THE MEN at D-Day—that was Robert Capa: daredevil, gambler, star photographer, storyteller, who probably added a few flourishes to his exploits. Experts may question the moment-by-moment details of these events. We can never know the full truth. But everyone agrees Capa was astonishingly brave. And yet behind the legend of Robert Capa is a penniless and scruffy young man.

Many years before, that young man and his girlfriend, Gerda Taro, along with their friends, set out to change the world with photographs. They would risk anything to reach people's hearts and show the world what photographs could do.

This is their story.

But like many stories, this one must loop back to the beginning—before the legend, before the fame—to a time when Capa and Taro must invent who they are.

A coastguardsman saw Capa "in the water, holding his cameras up to try to keep them dry" and calling for help. The ship, where medics were working on injured soldiers, picked up Capa and ferried him to the USS Samuel Chase, where he collapsed.

Leon Trotsky lost to Joseph Stalin in a struggle to lead the Soviet Union, and in 1929 he left the country. Trotsky remained a hero to many on the Left who disliked and distrusted Stalin. When André was given the assignment to photograph the dynamic speaker in Denmark in 1932, it was the photographer's first big break.

CHAPTER ONE

THE
ASSIGNMENT

PARIS, 1934

IF HE COULD JUST FIND THE GIRL.

André Friedmann pauses in front of La Coupole. He searches the faces of patrons sitting out on the terrace in cane chairs, drinking coffee and smoking cigarettes. André is dressed in a battered leather jacket, the same pair of trousers he wears every day, and old shoes whose soles are worn thin. No matter: he is handsome, with slicked-back black hair, twinkling eyes, and a ready, charming smile.

A small camera—a Leica—hangs on a thin strap around his neck. He carries a sheaf of photographs. Lucky for André the camera isn't in the pawnshop, where it often lands when he can't pay his bills. Money just leaks from André's pockets. There have been times when he has fled from an enraged landlady for not paying the rent, leaving his shoes and belongings behind. And he's always getting himself into awful fixes. Once, an assignment sent him down to the Riviera—the wealthy beach resort area in the south of France—where he not only burned through his budget but ruined a

André in Paris, taken in late 1934.
Photographer unknown.

borrowed camera by trying to shoot scenes underwater.

Today, André must find a girl—a model, that is—for a photography assignment. He desperately needs this job. Work is hard to come by these days. Paris, like the rest of France, the rest of Europe, and the United States, is suffering a terrible economic depression. It's not uncommon to see young men sleeping on benches, keeping themselves warm with flasks of whiskey, or scraping food off the pavement. Paris is charming, but not if you cannot eat.

There is a sense of crisis all over Europe. First the devastation of World War I, in which entire swaths of France, Belgium, and Germany were churned into mud from brutal battles, and a whole generation of young men were wounded or killed. Then the crippling Depression, with factories and stores shuttered and breadlines on the streets of every city. So-called democracy seems either a total failure or a complete fraud.

A mood of rage and blame hangs over the continent. Just last year, in 1933, Adolf Hitler was appointed the political leader of Germany. He promised to bring the German people "unity of mind and will" through shared racial bonds. In many German cities storm troopers roam the streets, beating up dissidents and slowly eliminating political opposition. In countries all across continental Europe—and even in England and the United States—political parties that describe Jews and communists as a kind of disease, an infection undermining the good people of the land, are gaining strength. But reports from the communist Soviet Union are also ominous. There are rumors that the government is deliberately keeping food from Ukrainian farmers, driving them to starvation.

André and his friends—nonconformists, leftists, Jews—are constantly on edge. No one knows where to go, where to live. A few are lucky enough to get visas to England or the United States, where they can start again. But the United States has strict limits on how many Jews it will admit, and its State Department officers so dislike Jews that they don't even fill the small quotas. Those who cannot leave Europe move around, trying one city after another.

Paris has become a city of refuge, where people fleeing Hitler and other dictators are safe for the moment. Not that it's easy to make a home here; a lot of Parisians don't like these newcomers. After all, many of the refugees speak German, and the French painfully remember their bloody battles with Germany during World War I just sixteen years before. And with French people out of work, no one wants outsiders taking jobs. So foreigners, exiles, are not allowed to work full-time. They must scrape by, as best they can, with freelance work, often relying on their own networks of friends and relations.

André got today's assignment from an old friend who told him of a Swiss

This photo captures the grim poverty in Paris. "Conditions in Paris have become terrible," André wrote to his nieces in February 1935, "and as aliens we are becoming less desirable by the minute."

insurance company that needed a photo of a German-looking girl with short blond hair and blue eyes. La Coupole, on the Left Bank, is where many of the German-speaking immigrants congregate. Like nearby Café du Dome, this café with its deep rows of cane chairs serves as a kind of home base for refugees and immigrants. Most live in tiny rooms and have little money and few possessions. Artists, writers, and photographers gather at the café to get tips about work, and talk and talk, mostly about politics.

Now André spots her: a slender, athletic-looking young woman with bobbed blond hair, chatting with a few other young women on the terrace. *Perfect!* he thinks, and rushes over to introduce himself.

Ruth Cerf, the blond girl, is not charmed. She eyes the scruffy young man with suspicion. *Strange*, she thinks. Sloppy, disheveled. Not appealing.

Still—maybe it's those dark eyes, or his disarming sense of humor; maybe she is flattered, or perhaps she feels sorry for him. He does look poor. And Ruth, who has come from Germany only a year ago, knows how hard it is to make a living here in Paris, especially as an immigrant. She even offers to buy him a cup of coffee, which he eagerly accepts. André explains he'd like her to pose for his assignment—they can meet at a nearby park, just blocks away. He pulls out a few of his photographs to show that he is serious, that this is not a con. Ruth is not sure—she does not want to be alone with a guy like this. Finally she agrees.

Ruth thinks: *I'll bring my roommate along as a chaperone. Just in case.*

ANDRÉ HAS ALWAYS BEEN A ROVER.

When he was a little boy growing up in Budapest, Hungary, he would wander about the city with his gang of friends, pulling pranks. In some ways, he took after his father, Dezső, who loved to tell the story of how he'd traveled around Europe as a young man using a menu as a fake passport. Dezső was also a gambler who spent the whole night at cafés playing cards with his friends. The family ran a tailoring business; after the economic crash in 1929, they operated out of their apartment, so André's home life was always haphazard. Thirty or forty employees streamed in and out of the apartment; sewing machines whirred until midnight. And as the family's business began to fail and they moved from place to place, collection agencies came knocking at the door to demand money for debts.

André's family was Jewish, but not particularly religious. Still, they were keenly aware of the rising danger to Jews. When André was six years old, gangs of anti-Semitic hooligans dragged Jews from their homes and from streetcars and beat them up. "Growing up in Budapest," a childhood friend of André's recalls, "one was constantly reminded of one's Jewishness. School arguments would often end by someone screaming 'you stinking Jew.'" By the time André was a young adult, Hungary was led by a dictator who was openly anti-Semitic. André developed a natural hatred toward anyone authoritarian or rule-bound. In his high school André always clashed with a rigid teacher, who would exclaim, "You are a cancer of the class!"

At seventeen, André and his friends joined a strike and protest march, which

Vu, *a French magazine aligned with the Left, made innovative use of photography and design and closely covered the rise of Hitler and fascism. This 1933 cover was created by Alexander Liberman, who later became a leading designer of fashion magazines in America.*

"The most charming boy I ever met but I didn't believe he would ever work," said friend and photographer Fred Stein of André, pictured here in a photo taken in 1935. Photographer unknown.

were forbidden by the government. By this time André had moved into leftist circles, even though he often joked, "The girls in the [Communist] Party are too ugly."

One night, the police showed up at the Friedmanns' door and took André away to prison, where he was beaten. Because the wife of the head of the secret police was a customer of his mother's, he was able to get out of jail, as long as he agreed to leave the country. André's worried mother put her son on a train to Vienna. From there, he would somehow make his way to Germany.

There, in the drizzly streets of Berlin, Germany's capital, with very little money, André began to immerse himself in photography, working as a dark-room assistant and errand boy for Dephot, a photo service. Dephot, like other agencies, served as a kind of clearinghouse for photographs. Photographers would bring in their images, which would then be sold to publications all over Europe and sometimes in America, too. During this period, picture agencies offered one of the very few pathways for refugees such as André to scratch out a living.

Soon André was carrying equipment, and then taking on assignments himself and showing talent. He continued to move in leftist political circles, still with a whiff of the teenage prankster. On cold nights, André and his friends would pour buckets of water onto the streets in the hopes that the Nazis who marched past in their black boots would slip and fall.

But by 1933, when Hitler was appointed chancellor, André began to see brown-shirted thugs assaulting Jews and leftists on the streets of Berlin. He knew it was time to leave. He and his child-hood friend Cziki Weisz made their way to Paris.

Ominous news from Germany followed him. Shortly after André left Berlin, Hitler's regime began enacting laws against Jews, who were forbidden to hold

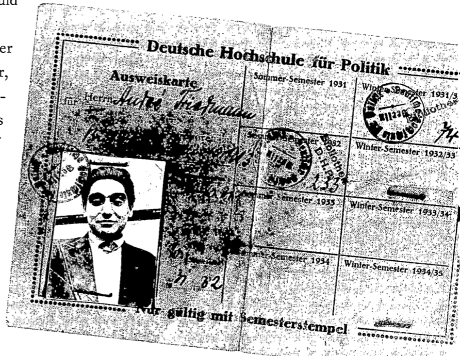

André's identity card, issued in Berlin in 1931.

any public-service jobs or work in professions such as the law. Jewish professors and students were forced to leave their universities. They were forbidden even to appear onstage or in movies.

PARIS MIGHT BE A HAVEN, but for how long? Flickering on screens in movie theaters are newsreels of the dictator thrusting his arm out in the Nazi salute, declaring his ambitions to conquer more of Europe, the world. Crackling over the Bakelite radios, shouting from a balcony in Rome, come the speeches of Italian dictator Benito Mussolini, whose army is threatening to invade Ethiopia. The Japanese have taken over Manchuria. The League of Nations—the last hope for finding world peace—seems doomed as it can do nothing to halt either Mussolini or the Japanese. Everyone fears a new world war is imminent.

André stays focused on his pictures. They are his ticket to survival. If his shots are good—not too blurred and rushed, as they sometimes are—then he will be able to earn enough francs to pay off his debts. He will get through just one more day.

Fortunately, the photography session with Ruth Cerf is a success. She poses on a bench in a little park, her blond hair shining in the sunlight. Ruth photographs well—she has wide eyes and a large, sensuous mouth; her beauty has helped her to land several modeling jobs. Yet the whole time, it is actually Ruth's vivacious, red-haired friend who catches André's eye.

Ruth's friend looks like a silent movie star, and she knows it. Her eyebrows are plucked, giving her foxlike face a startled look, like the famous actress Greta Garbo. She looks like a girl who knows how to stretch her francs and carry herself with flair—she wears berets cocked just so on her hair, dyed red with henna. A friend describes her as "beautiful, like a little deer, with big eyes, auburn hair, and fine features."

He learns her name: Gerta Pohorylle.

GERTA WAS ALWAYS DETERMINED. She grew up in Stuttgart, Germany, where her father was a Jewish grocer selling dairy goods. He made enough money to give his daughter a nice middle-class childhood. She enjoyed fashionable clothes, went to a girls' school with other German children, spent one year at a Swiss boarding school, played tennis, and, in her teen years, had a dashing boyfriend.

In 1929, when she was nineteen, her family moved to Leipzig. Her father's business began to falter. Gerta was now drawn to politics. She joined the local Socialist Workers' Party, as did her brothers, and all three siblings were soon active in anti-Nazi activities, including a leafleting campaign.

A glamorous image of Gerta taken by an unknown photographer in Paris.

One day in 1933 her two brothers dared to scatter anti-Nazi pamphlets from the roof of a department store. Immediately, they fled into hiding. Hoping to pressure the family, the authorities arrested Gerta, who arrived at the jail dressed in a bright checked skirt. Even in prison, Gerta never lost her lightheartedness. She spent several weeks locked up, developing friendships with the other inmates and passing the time by singing American jazz songs. She also displayed a hint of her steely bravery and sharp mind—tapping in code on the prison walls to communicate with others, crying in front of an official in order to soften his heart and secure her release.

By the time she was set free from prison, Gerta knew she must leave Germany as soon as possible. And so, like André, like thousands of other young people, many of them Jewish, in October 1933 she rushed to Paris.

Those early days in Paris! Gerta and her best friend, Ruth, who had come a few months before, roomed together. Gerta picked up a bit of work, but they had so little money that their stomachs gnawed with hunger. On weekends, they'd stay in their room and huddle under the quilt in their one bed, just to conserve energy. Or they'd head over to a café, where they'd play a trick: grabbing a

Fred Stein captured this image of the well-groomed young woman.

croissant from a huge basket on the bar, they quickly ate half of it, signaling to the waiter to charge them and also order a drink. When the waiter turned his back, they would wolf down the rest of the croissant, then eat half of another.

For a brief while, she and Ruth roomed with Fred Stein and his wife, Liselotte, who had an enormous apartment with extra bedrooms. Fred had originally studied to be a lawyer in Berlin, but when he was unable to practice under Nazi law, he too picked up a camera and was making a go of it professionally.

What good parties they all had there—putting colored bulbs in the lamps, dancing! Fred snapped pictures of Gerta, mugging away. Yes, being poor, a stranger in a strange city, was awful, but to have the solace of friends, all in the same situation, made it easier. Maybe that's why, as Ruth put it, "we were all of the Left." That is, they belonged to a loose collection of groups opposed to fascism and in favor of workers' rights.

Gerta was never exactly a joiner. Her sympathies, her ideas, came from her years in Leipzig. She hated the Nazis and knew how dangerous it was becoming for her family. But she wasn't one of those who debated every political point. She wasn't part of the Communist Party, which took its direction from the Soviet Union. But she did care about social issues, about the future ahead. They all did.

For now, there was food and coffee at the Café du Dome and talk with friends. And photographs. Above all, photographs.

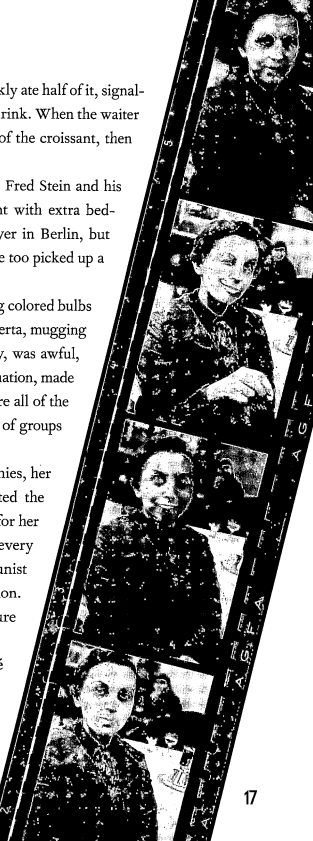

Gerta mugs for the camera.
Probably taken by André.

This picture of Gerta and André at the Café du Dôme, near their apartment, was taken in 1935 by Fred Stein, who was also a regular at the café.

CHAPTER TWO

COMPLETELY IN LOVE

FALL 1934–SPRING 1936

FROM THE START, Gerta treats André as a friend, a pal, a kind of project. In the undisciplined, lovably boyish André, she sees an enormous talent for photography. She shows André how to groom himself, gives him tips on how to present himself to magazines, and critiques his story ideas. In a way, she "professionalizes" him and makes him get serious about his photography.

During this time, André's feelings for Gerta begin to shift. He becomes more dependent on her—especially as there are many ups and downs in his life: though he gets assignments and sells pictures, half his projects fizzle out, and he can barely make ends meet. Still he dreams. Gerta becomes more attached to him, though she seems to think of him still as a friend, her *copain*—comrade and colleague—whose talent she believes in.

In April, even though André lands an assignment in Spain, his spirits sink to a new low. Always the more emotional of the two, he confesses to Gerta that "in Madrid I felt I had become a nobody." He ends his letter with

Fred Stein captured Gerta the hard-working career girl in this 1935 photo.

a tentative confession, reaching out to the girl who is starting to steady his ambitions: "Sometimes, I am, nevertheless, completely in love with you."

That summer Gerta and André join a group of friends and camp out in the ruins of an old fortress in the south of France. It is a glorious two months' adventure. They eat makeshift meals, swim in the warm waters of the Mediterranean, snap pictures. They leave all their troubles behind: they are not Jews, worried about a landlady who might be a Nazi sympathizer. They are not refugees without proper papers, fretting about their family. They are not running or desperate. They are just like any other young people, carefree, lighthearted. They build campfires, flirt, their eyes shining in the firelight.

And they fall in love.

In autumn, André and Gerta move into a one-room apartment near the Eiffel Tower and set up a new life together. "Imagine, Mother," André writes home, "my hair is short, my tie is hanging on my neck, my shoes are shined, and I appear on the scene at seven o'clock. And what is more surprising, in the evening at nine, I am already at home. In one word, it is the end of the bohemian life."

Gerta gets a new job working for Maria Eisner, who runs Alliance Photo, an agency that distributes photographs to newspapers and magazines all over Europe. With dramatic events swirling throughout the world, the demand for photographs is high. Selling photos is an excellent way for an outsider to get her footing in a foreign country.

André proudly tells his mother, "Considering that she is even more intelligent than she is pretty, the results are great, and the firm is selling six times as many photographs as they had previously."

Work, love, friends, photography—it is all intertwined. Gerta advises André, types up the captions for his photographs, and sells them to her boss. She also makes André wear a blazer and tie, so that he makes a better impression on editors. Nor is Gerta one to hold back on criticism. "She does not put a lock on her mouth if she does not like something," he sighs to his mother in a letter.

Not that André is complaining. Since Gerta came into his life, he is more stable and focused. Sure, they cram into a skinny bed together and are lucky if they get five, six hours of sleep. She rises before him, just as the early morning's light peeks through the window, to get dressed in front of the tiny mirror.

"Ragged one," he teases her, since she has to conceal holes in her clothes. "The good girl she is," he writes his mother, "introduces me to every editor, helps me a great deal, and writes articles besides. On the other hand, she not only doesn't darn my socks, she does not do anything about the holes in her stockings."

By seven, she's rushing out the door to get to the office. He stays behind, tidies up, washes the breakfast dishes, and "proceeds to break all the glasses." Then he spends all day out on the street, hustling to get assignments, hoping to sell his pictures.

Gerta works side by side in the tiny office with Maria Eisner. She types and organizes photographs and is on the phone with publications. Thank goodness her father had thought to send her to a finishing school in Switzerland, for her knowledge of French and German, and just a bit of Spanish, has come in handy. Most recently, she's been reading *Nineteen Nineteen*, a novel by the American writer John Dos Passos, to teach herself English. Bent over the typewriter, with her plucked eyebrows and the determined jut of her chin, Gerta is the essence of a career girl—self-willed and canny. She is "extremely ambitious," André's childhood friend Cziki Weisz observes, and is keen "to be famous."

André has begun to teach Gerta how to take photographs. Just as she helped André with his appearance, he trains her in how to aim the camera and frame a shot. This is the basis of their relationship—an exchange, a partnership, sharing their individual strengths and know-how. In art, women often serve as the muse for the male artist, the beauty who is photographed or painted. But André and Gerta are breaking new ground: they both are involved in the creation of the work. Their professional and personal lives are completely intertwined. André is the bold, intuitive risk taker, chasing after assignments. Gerta is lightly flirtatious, charming, with a clear sense of goals and how to present oneself to the world. They respect each other as equals, casting off traditional notions of man and woman, artist and subject, even husband and wife.

"Never before in my life have I been so happy!" André tells his beloved mentor, André Kertész, another Hungarian photographer. "Now only the pick and the spade [the grave] could separate Gerta and me."

THE RUSE

Imagine: You are young. You have nothing. How hard can it be to shed your old self and become someone new?

There is one big way André and Gerta can make their luck change—their names. No one knows exactly who decided on the name change, but bets are on the savvy Gerta, with her eye for style and illusion. Together they come up with a scheme to land more lucrative photography jobs. Gerta will pretend she is trying to sell the photographs of a famous and rich American photographer named Robert Capa, who will offer his images for no less than 150 francs. She too will change her name: Gerta Pohorylle will become Gerda Taro—fascinatingly similar to Greta Garbo. Their new names give them an alluring, glamorous air. As Capa writes his mother about his new name, "One could almost say that I've been born again, but this time it didn't cause anyone any pain."

There is another side to their name change. The situation for Jews is getting worse. At the Nazis' Nuremberg rally in September 1935, Jews were declared unfit for citizenship in the Reich. With anti-Semitism on the rise and Paris increasingly hostile to foreigners, the couple wants to erase any sign of a particular nation, religion, or identity. Their new names are a disguise, a protection, "a farewell to any fixed point in the world, to any country."

This Vu *cover reads: "At the Nuremberg Rally: The Apotheosis of Might." The image of robotic soldiers conveys the sense of the growing Nazi threat.*

The ruse is a daring move. Every time someone asks to meet the elusive Robert Capa, Gerda hedges, saying he is busy traveling, and offers to send his dark-haired assistant "André" instead. Maria Eisner is suspicious when she sees the photographs Gerda shows her. She's sure they're Friedmann's, but she decides to hold her tongue.

Besides, "Robert's" photographs are more and more in demand—especially as politics are heating up.

Capa's photo of the May Day celebrations shows the massive crowds,
marching and waving flags, that poured into the Place de la République.
Many demonstrations continue to be held in the same spot, creating a haunting
connection between the political passions of the 1930s and those of today.

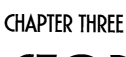

CHAPTER THREE

A STORY
IN PICTURES

PARIS, SPRING 1936

MAY DAY—the symbolic day when workers around the world march and show unity. André and Gerta—now Robert Capa and Gerda Taro—are hurrying the few short blocks from their new, tiny apartment at the Hotel de Blois to meet friends at the Café du Dome. Together, they will take the metro across town to join the May Day celebrations at Place de la République.

   This May Day is especially charged, as elections will take place in two days. And the vote is not just about France—it is symbolic for all of Europe, which is now waging a war of ideas. What is the way forward? Which ideas, what plan, can save the world? Is it communism, led by Joseph Stalin and the Soviet Union, which promises a workers' paradise? To those who treasure the writing of Karl Marx, the Depression is simply to be expected—visible proof that capitalism is doomed. As one American puts it, "At the very moment when our own country, to the surprise of all except the Marxists,

*The sequence of photos here through page 28, pages 30–33, and page 35 are Capa's images of
political demonstrations in 1936 and 1937. This photo was taken at a fascist rally in 1936;
the raised arms in the other images, beginning on page 27, are the sign of the Popular Front.*

was sliding into a social-economic abyss, the new social system of the Russian workers and peasants showed striking gains."

What about socialism, a modified, softer version of communism? Is this the answer? Or fascism, which offers an image of manly strength and unity? The term *fascist* comes from ancient Rome's *fascis*; it means a bundle of sticks tightly bound together. The fascists claim that all of the divisions in a nation—rich and poor, left and right—will fall away when the nation unites behind a powerful leader. The twentieth century, Mussolini proudly announces, is to be a "fascist century."

Socialists, communists, fascists all believe in an ever stronger government. Anarchists think just the opposite. They want to eliminate central government entirely so that people would live in small collectives where their voices could be heard and where all would work together for the good of all.

Strong leader or no leader? Communism or socialism? Fascism or anarchism? Young people everywhere reach for these ideologies, yearning to see the world repaired. Every one of these movements is tempting because it promises a total solution: wipe away the old, diseased past and create a brand-new, modern future. Everyone is marching; everyone is declaring that they and only they have

Taken in Paris, 1936.

Taken in Paris, 1936 or 1937.

the answer to the world's crippling troubles.

Not far behind the speeches is the rumble of violence—skirmishes between armed factions on the streets and, even more ominous, armies training, nations preparing for war.

All through the spring of 1936, this clash fills the streets of Paris. The Soviet Union has ordered communist parties throughout the world to put aside their differences with the socialists and join forces in a new coalition, the Popular Front, which promises sweeping reforms. The decision of the socialists and communists to form a common alliance is like rivals in a playground deciding to band together to fight the bigger bully of fascism, which is threatening to take over. For Capa and Taro, for all the young people who are worried about the future, this election and the promise of the Popular Front represent a moment of hope. This is the time to unite and defeat the true enemy—fascism. Every weekend brings another Popular Front march.

These are especially heady times for Capa. In April his good friend Chim, another, more established photographer, went off to Spain to cover the new Popular Front government that was just barely elected in February. (No one can pronounce David Szymin's name, so he goes by Chim.) Before leaving, Chim told his editors to hire Capa to cover the similar Popular Front movement in France. So Capa is busier than ever with more assignments, enthusiastically snapping pictures. Maria Eisner has also hired him on a regular basis with a small stipend. Week after

This page from a Belgian socialist publication shows the "new hope" of the Popular Front. Chim took the image of the hopeful crowd at a land reform rally in Spain. See another photo he took then, and how it was used, on pages 104–105.

Two men ride on a Popular Front float in a May Day parade in Paris in 1936 or 1937.
Capa may have taken the shot because the word Bresson *in the store sign reminded him*
of his friend and fellow photographer Henri Cartier-Bresson.

week as the election nears, Capa is at the demonstrations, capturing the mood
and starting to show real flair and swagger as a photographer.

Sometimes Capa teeters from a rooftop to capture a sea of heads, protesters
bearing antifascist banners or signs exhorting people to fight anti-Semitism. Or
he plunges into crowds, homing in on an individual: a little boy in a one-piece
woolen suit raising his fist in the Popular Front salute, imitating the adults around

him. Or elegant old men in a car, deep in conversation, or people at a rally, heads craned upward, listening intently to speeches. His images show how on edge, how riveted, everyone is. Though the Popular Front is gaining ground, there are battles with the extreme right, which is emboldened by the regimes of Germany and Italy. No one can tell, exactly, where the current of events will take them.

Today at the Café du Dome, Chim has recently returned from Spain. There the Popular Front's hold on power appears to be fragile. Spasms of violence broke out when some on the left went on destructive rampages. And there have been rumblings from the military and factions on the right who do not accept the Left's vision for Spain. They see communism as a foreign disease, an infection from the Soviet Union that must be purged so that order, Christianity, and monarchy will be restored.

Chim wears his trademark three-piece suit, peering at the passersby through wire-rimmed spectacles while he carefully sips his coffee. Originally from Poland, Chim could not be more opposite from Capa. While Capa is a scruffy, charming boy, loudly joking with everyone at the table, Chim is more like a reserved, old-fashioned professor. "Chim thought about everything very deeply. He had a personality a bit

Taken at the Place de la République on May 1, 1936 or 1937. This is a close-up of the enthusiastic crowds at protests— even taking over the base of a statue.

*Young and old, perhaps father and son, at a
Popular Front rally in Paris, October 1936.*

like that of a rabbi. And the mind of a mathemati-
cian or chess player," explains their friend and fellow photographer Henri Cartier-Bresson. "He felt
the weight of Jewish tradition on his shoulders."
Despite these differences, a deep affection and
respect courses between the two men, and they
influence each other as photographers.

When the friends emerge into the Place de la
République, Capa leaves the others on the side-
walk and rushes into the street. The crowds are
huge, converging on the central square from all
directions like the seething spokes of a wheel.

Capa doesn't wait; he clambers up lamp poles
to shoot the surging crowd. He swings his camera upward, revealing young men watching be-
musedly from the top of a shop awning. A swarm
of supporters stand at the base of a statue in
the center of the square. Children sit atop their
fathers' shoulders. Young, old, mothers,
grandparents—a human river flows down the
broad boulevards.

There is Capa, moving swiftly, "crouching,"
a fellow photographer notices, "and watching like a cat . . . waiting for his
chance to spring his picture, sidling up, insinuating himself, not attracting attention to himself, head bent over camera, completely absorbed in his job."

Many news photographers take pictures of the crowds walking down streets
with their arms raised in the characteristic salute of the Popular Front, but Capa's
more personal shots let us into the truth of these events. Out of the numbing

parade of arms and legs, the blur of faces, he is able to seize on the particular, the human, the one shot that tells the whole story: a child, atop the father's shoulders, waving a French flag.

Capa is already developing his trademark eye. This is what will distinguish his work and that of his circle in the years to come. As big movements and big ideas sweep the streets, the entire continent of Europe, he homes in on what it means to be human during such momentous times.

He is beginning to tell a story. A story in pictures.

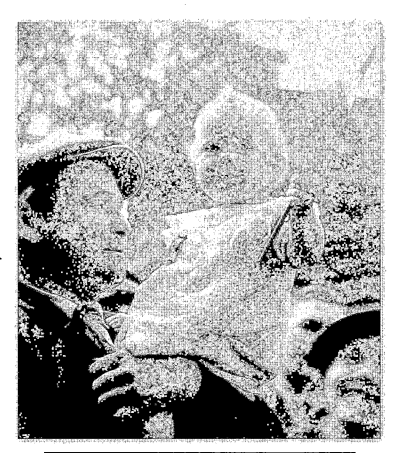

Capa looks for ways to make a massive march in Paris, 1936, a very human expression of hope, as in this image of what must be a father and his young child.

THE WORLD IN BLACK AND WHITE

Why is photography so tempting for Capa and his friends?

In the nineteenth century, when the camera came into use, it was a clumsy box that needed to sit on top of a stand or tripod. The photographer would slide a large glass plate into the back of the camera. Subjects had to stay frozen, often for more than a few seconds, while the photographer dipped his head under a curtain. Then he squeezed the shutter button while a lightbulb he held with his other hand popped, stunning the eyes with its blinding flash. That's why early photographs look like static paintings. Action shots were nearly impossible.

Over time, the old camera boxes became smaller and a little more portable. Eastman Kodak's Brownie camera, introduced in 1900, was made of cardboard and was so small and simple a child could use it. There was also the Rolleiflex, a long box with a viewfinder on the top that you stared into to see the image floating inside.

For all cameras, after the images were captured, the film was laboriously developed: dipped in chemicals to create negatives, which were then put in an enlarger. The resulting image was exposed to special light-sensitive paper. Slowly, slowly, the submerged sheets were soaked in tubs of chemicals, tapped with tongs, until the prints emerged like ghostly traces.

In the 1920s and 1930s, a German firm revolutionized photography by creating the portable Leica. The Contax camera, developed by a competitor, followed shortly after. These cameras were small and rested snugly in your palm. They used thirty-five-millimeter film—the same size used in movies—which was inserted on a left spool with sprockets and threaded across to the right spool. With each click, the shutter opened and the image was exposed on a rectangle of film. The photographer then advanced to the next frame. The mechanisms inside were fast: you could click away and capture action in less than a second. It was like taking a movie of many stills, getting every beat, every moment in an event.

Now Capa, Taro, and others can move around, lift the camera to the eye, focus, and shoot, again and again.

The Leica IIIb was introduced in 1938 but was very similar to the camera Capa would have used.

*To Capa's camera, some strikes—such as this one, photographed
in 1936 or 1937— were more joyous fun than grim protest.*

These new cameras are like everything that is happening in the twentieth
century: sleek, modern, lightweight.

And they are perfect for yet another new invention: the photographic news
magazine. Just as politics and events are turning more turbulent and as modern
life speeds up, these illustrated magazines are being consumed by millions of
readers across Europe. They are part of a new, kinetic, and connected world,

where news feels nearly instant. The publications cover not just big events but everyday happenings, fashions, trends. People are seeing their own lives mirrored back to them through images. Readers everywhere hunger for photographs of the here and now.

For Capa, who craves action and adventure, the lightweight camera and the photography-filled magazines are a perfect fit. The camera becomes an extension of his body, his eye; it becomes a way of taking in the fast-moving events. If you can pick up a camera, aim, and shoot, you are part of the current of the now.

That is why so many of these young people have taken up the medium. Capa's good friend Henri Cartier-Bresson is the only one in his and Gerda's social circle who is not a refugee or an immigrant; he comes from a wealthy French family. Originally he studied painting and literature, until he, too, caught the photography bug, capturing fleeting moments that are somehow the essence of Parisian life. Tall and bookish, an intellectual who reads the communist

*Strikes took place around France, and Capa recorded
workers sitting on the rooftop of the Galeries Lafayette
department store in June 1936, and in the same year,
sleeping on a factory floor and receiving packages of food.*

newspaper every morning, Cartier-Bresson makes an unlikely friend for Capa. But the two relish each other's company and can often be found at a café discussing politics or swapping tips about assignments. It is Capa who urges his friend to leave the rarefied world of art: "Call yourself a photojournalist," he tells him, "and then do whatever you like."

For immigrants, photography is a way to gain a foothold in their new surroundings. Says fellow Hungarian Ata Kandó: "It was a job immigrants could take on without having to speak the language well."

JULY 1936, MOROCCO AND SPAIN

Short, pale, and with a round belly, General Francisco Franco does not seem like the most dynamic leader to spearhead a military coup. But for four years he has brought victories to Spain, fighting to keep control of Spanish Morocco. He is ambitious, cold, pragmatic, and even manages to win the respect of the Moroccans he defeated. Ever since the new Popular Front government was elected in Spain, the military has been plotting to overthrow it.

"Everyone in his senses knew," wrote a government army officer, "that Spain, far from being a happy and blissful country, was living on a volcano."

On July 17, 1936, military troops storm government offices and seize control of Spanish Morocco. By the next day, the Canary Islands, which sit off the Atlantic coast of northwestern Africa, are taken. General Franco immediately flies to the city of Tetuán in Spanish Morocco, where he is met by a crowd of enthusiastic rebel officers.

Bedecked in his uniform with tasseled epaulets and a sash across the chest, Franco declares, "At stake is the need to restore the empire of ORDER within the REPUBLIC . . . and the principle of AUTHORITY."

Civil war erupts. In Barcelona, fighting immediately breaks out on the streets as groups defending the Popular Front government grab weapons and try to repel the military rebels.

That night, Dolores Ibárruri, a fiery orator and a Communist Party leader, gets on the radio and gives an impassioned speech. "Workers! Farmers! Antifascists! Spanish patriots! Confronted with the fascist military uprising, all must rise to their feet, to defend the Republic, to defend the people's freedoms as well as their achievements toward democracy!" La Pasionaria (the passion flower), as Ibárruri is known, then sounds the battle cry for the loyalists who defend the Republic: "Long live the Popular Front! Long live the union of all antifascists! Long live the Republic of the people! The fascists shall not pass! THEY SHALL NOT PASS!"

By July 19, the summer music that usually blares from loudspeakers in Barcelona has changed to speeches and exhortations to rise up and fight Franco's rebels. Workers stream onto La Rambla, the main walkway in Barcelona, to join rapidly forming militias that will fight Franco's men. The worst of the fighting takes place at the Atarazanas barracks, the main military stronghold, near the port. After three days, the military rebels are driven back. For those on the left, for the workers and peasants especially, Franco's military uprising is a call to arms. This isn't just a civil war—it's a chance to completely make over Spain.

This poster shows values the rebels associated with their cause and with Franco, who became their leader: honor, heroism, faith, authority, justice, efficiency, intelligence, will, and austerity.

Revolution springs up everywhere. In Barcelona, the tram lines and telephone systems are quickly taken over by political parties. In villages and towns, new committees are created, with a complete reorganization of who is in charge. In the region of Aragon, farms are swiftly turned into collectives. In some parts of Catalonia, even money is

Hitler planned the 1936 Olympics in Berlin to be a display of German might and Aryan superiority. In response, antifascists on the left created a People's Olympics to be held in Barcelona. The American team was selected to be racially integrated and to feature working-class athletes. The rebellion against the Republic broke out on July 19, just as the games were to start, and they were soon canceled.

eliminated. In Madrid, restaurants serve free meals of rice and potatoes, boiled with meat.

For everyone watching Spain from afar, the Republic's battle against Franco is a line in the sand. It's the chance to resist fascism and stop the greater war they fear is looming on the not-so-distant horizon.

"When the fighting broke out on 18 July," an English writer noted, "it is probable that every antifascist in Europe felt a thrill of hope. For here at last, apparently, was democracy standing up to fascism. For years past the so-called democratic countries had been surrendering to fascism at every step. . . . But when Franco tried to overthrow a mildly left-wing government, the Spanish people, against all expectation, had risen against him. It seemed— possibly it was—the turning of the tide."

As Chim would write a friend, "Dear boy, the world is not doing well, but it will be better and soon. It nears, we can feel it, we can see it, and it hangs in the air."

PARIS

For Taro and Capa, the news from Spain is a chance, an opportunity. They decide they must immediately go to Spain—together, as a team—and capture these vital events.

Before they leave, they visit a friend who feeds them breakfast and notices that "they were deeply in love, and she was so happy to go there with him. They were as broke as ever, and I did what I could and made them a meal."

The trip to Spain is a big change in their relationship, an open declaration of their partnership. It is a major step for Taro, who is not just on the sidelines, aiding and helping Capa. She now has a press pass and is declaring herself to be a photographer in her own right. Yet Spain is a gamble. They are still new at this—who knows what work they'll be able to sell?

To Capa and Taro, to everyone, this war is not just about Spain—this is the struggle of their generation. This is a war that will determine the fate of Europe and whether it will indeed fall under the dark spell of fascism. A reporter for the Soviet newspaper *Pravda* describes the struggle for Spain as going "far beyond the trenches of Madrid; it goes right through Europe, through the whole world."

The *New York Times* reporter Herbert Matthews sees what the conflict in Spain means to young people: "This world will not be worth living in if fascism triumphs."

Capa and Taro are going to use the new technology—their lightweight cameras—to capture the story, to win over good souls everywhere, to be the eyes of the world. To support the Spanish Republic is a kind of claim, a cross between a passionate wish and a firm declaration. Capa and Taro know, with searing certainty, the danger of fascism; they have experienced it firsthand. If Spain can stand against the generals, fascism everywhere can be defeated. And so the two young, newly anointed photographers board a plane that Vogel has hired to get them and other journalists there.

First stop: Barcelona.

VU EN ESPAGNE

la défense de la République

This August 1936 Vu cover captures the energy of the citizens who rose up to defend the Republic against the rebel armies.

CHAPTER FOUR

FIRST STOP: REVOLUTION

AUGUST 1936

IT IS AUGUST in Barcelona, an elegant city perched on the blue Mediterranean Sea. The air is hot, muggy, still. Capa and Taro have come to shoot a war. Instead they find a living revolution.

Capa and Taro's purpose is to show Spain to the world through their cameras, bringing this war to the eyes of magazine readers through-out Europe and beyond. The magazine *Vu* has sent them, but they have no salary; they will earn only as much money as the pictures they sell. Even getting their photos back to Paris editors can be risky and challenging. They

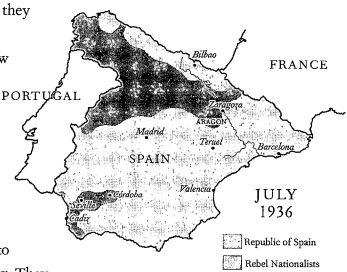

FRANCE

PORTUGAL

Bilbao

Zaragoza

ARAGON

Madrid

Teruel

Barcelona

SPAIN

Córdoba

Valencia

Seville

Cadiz

JULY 1936

Republic of Spain

Rebel Nationalists

must always be alert, finding out when another journalist or a courier is heading back to Paris and can take a package of their prints or negatives to an editor or agency. Taro is being especially daring, since no woman has ever gone into a combat zone to take photographs. But they know that readers, especially those on the left, are hungry for news and images. They hope to find the strong Spanish standing up against fascism, the people united to defeat the grim generals.

Quickly the two gain their bearings, amazed at all the ways the city has been transformed. Barcelona is cosmopolitan and modern: white stone apartment buildings with wrought iron balconies look out on promenades that are shaded by the thick foliage of palm and plane trees. Barcelona's fiercely independent residents speak not Spanish but Catalan—a separate language descended directly from Latin. Every major political party in the rest of Spain has a local affiliate here that uses Catalan and has its own ideas. The Catalans are not just interested in defeating Franco; they aim to transform their own lives, shedding centuries-old customs and structures of power. Barcelona has turned into a revolutionary dream.

The Hotel Ritz, which used to cater only to the wealthy, is now a place for free meals. Its fancy lobby is filled with long tables where, all day, residents come in to eat. Factories and stores have been taken over by workers; private property has been confiscated. All cars now belong to the government in order to serve the war effort. Local trams and taxis are painted black—the color of anarchism. Free public schools and nurseries have been opened for all children, ending the Catholic

Taro makes this August 1936 send-off to the front look more like good-byes before a vacation. The photos by Taro and Capa through page 53 were all taken that month in Barcelona.

Church's long domination of education. No one wears business suits anymore; bankers and plumbers put on the same one-piece canvas coveralls. Even language has changed. Traditional Spanish and Catalan require a person to speak deferentially to those of high status and informally to social inferiors. Now *señor* and *doña* and the formal *usted* have been abandoned; everyone is addressed the same way, as *compadre*, comrade.

Barcelona is "startling and overwhelming," writes a young man named Eric Blair, who uses the pen name George Orwell. He is thrilled at the mood of the city. "It was the first time that I had ever been in a town where the working class was in the saddle. Practically every building of any size had been seized by the workers and was draped with red flags or with the red-and-black flag of the anarchists; every wall was scrawled with the hammer and sickle and with the initials of the revolutionary parties."

As Capa and Taro roam the Barcelona streets, they're soon caught up in the spirit of the place. Their photographs capture the city's mood of hope, excitement, and limitless possibility. Their lenses find the joyous spirit in which residents have taken up arms and are remaking their society: soldiers gladly loading bread into a truck or passing guns to new recruits. Smiling young men look out a window cracked from an earlier battle. Little boys happily scamper on sandbagged walls, donning anarchist caps like any

Taro captures three relaxed men at the headquarters of a Catalan Communist Party and boys using sandbags as a playground. In these images, she sees a mood of hope and joy in revolutionary Barcelona.

Taro's image of a child and his soldier father at a bullfight
in Barcelona is about family instead of war.

children playing war games. Father and son cheer a bullfight and rally presented by one of the Left parties. All around are signs of this living revolution.

Taro especially is pleased to see women wearing practical clothes: the trademark blue coveralls and rope-soled shoes, called *alpargatas*, or trousers and men's shirts and ties. Young women strolling up and down streets wearing blue coveralls or sitting unaccompanied in cafés is remarkable in conservative Spain, which sees a woman's place as confined to the home. "When we went into the villages, people would say, 'A woman in trousers!'" one anarchist woman says. "My parents kicked me out of the house for wearing trousers."

Soon Taro dresses like the other liberated women—baggy pants cinched with a belt, rope shoes, her hair cut spikey short. Her tomboy look makes it easier to shoot and maneuver around. Though she is using a Reflex-Korelle, where one must look down into the viewfinder to frame a shot, she manages the camera with no trouble; Taro is "small but enormously strong and fit, so the size of the camera didn't require any effort."

Using Taro's contacts from the German socialist party and her modest knowledge of Spanish, the young couple make their way to the headquarters of POUM, the Partido Obrero de Unificación Marxista. The Workers Party of Marxist Unification is a popular and independent-minded communist group fiercely opposed to Stalin and dead set against following the lead of the Soviet Union. Its ideas are similar to the views she heard and shared with groups in Germany and then Paris.

On a beach next to the lapping Mediterranean, Taro crouches in the sand and photographs loyalist militiawomen training. She shows women proudly conferring with one another, dressed in uniforms with leather ammunition cartridges pinned to their belts. One of her most famous shots shows a silhouetted woman taking aim with her pistol. That photo and the others will be used in a two-page spread for *Vu* to show how women are a part of this historic struggle.

Women in Spain had never been allowed to fight with weapons; no one

This has become one of Taro's most famous photos—a young Spanish woman taking up arms to fight for a new kind of Spain.

could even imagine them as soldiers or in the police force. In revolutionary Barcelona, that has changed. This woman is unlike any woman seen in Spain before; she is a symbol of power, strength, and independence—a young woman fiercely in charge.

Many of Taro's pictures of the loyalist militia are taken slightly from below, which makes each figure look tall and imposing in the photograph. Under the open summer sunlight, their faces are strong and molded; one sees the angles of their noses, the defined jaws, the squinting eyes that gaze out at the horizon. Her shots depict the common people as warriors, larger than life, idealized. The troops may be ragtag, with mismatched uniforms, rusty rifles, and a mix of caps, black berets, and helmets, but they are unified in their heroism, their unwavering sense of purpose. This is a *people's* army.

This documentary photo from Madrid shows the poster war—images on every possible surface advertised one political party or another.

Capa and Taro are in Spain to educate the eyes of the rest of Europe, but there is also a clash of images going on right in front of them. Every wall, building, and passing car tells a story in scrawled graffiti, dramatic posters, and blazing colors. "The revolutionary posters were everywhere, flaming from the walls in clean reds and blues that made the few remaining advertisements look like daubs of mud," Orwell observes. The posters are intense propaganda, since in Spain at this time, 40 percent of women and 25 percent of men cannot read or write. In the countryside, the numbers are as high as 90 percent.

The vivid posters speak as loudly as bullhorns, proclaiming the message of the revolution—and recruiting bodies to fight on the front. Mujeres Libres, an anarchist organization for women, advertises its cause by depicting a woman in a long gown thrusting both arms in the air as she faces a row of guns. Other posters show fighters, muscled men grasping rifles, all with blaring, colorful headlines. The heroism of the posters can be felt everywhere. Orwell heard loudspeakers "bellowing revolutionary songs all day and far into the night." Everywhere there is the slogan of the Republic: *No pasarán*, they shall not pass.

Despite the steady drumbeat of recruiting and training and news of guns crackling hundreds of miles away, many of the pictures Capa and Taro take during their first weeks in Spain show festive, happy people. At the Barcelona train station, a soldier embraces his wife before he swings onto the departing train. A group of soldiers clamber onto one another like a football huddle, grinning—all with their arms raised in the Popular Front salute. War is a kind of grand and lighthearted party. Even the little bit of military action shown—sandbagged trenches, marching— reflects a hopeful city preparing to defend itself.

Equality, community—surely this is what excites Taro and Capa. Perhaps they see something of themselves in these young people volunteering and marching off to war. Their photos almost vibrate with a sense of adventure and common purpose. Here is a city filled with men and women trying to forge a new way of living. Barcelona captures

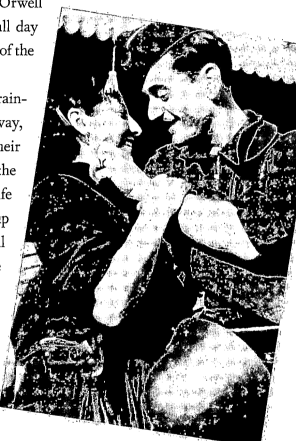

A good-bye between a man and a woman. Notice that she, too, carries a gun in a holster, exemplifying the ideal of equality between men and women during this period. This photo by Capa echoes Taro's photo of the kneeling woman.

Capa records the jubilant leave-taking of soldiers on a train to the front.

the yearnings, hopes, and dreams they exchanged over stolen pastries in the Paris cafés. Perhaps there is a wish behind these pictures: *be safe, win, stop the fascists—and we will all be safe.*

One of Taro's best images is of a man and a woman leaning back in two wicker chairs, heads tilted to each other, exchanging laughter. The man casually holds a rifle between them. There's an easy grace to the photo—men and women as comfortable compadres. Capa photographs the very same couple, at the same moment, from a slightly different angle, though it is Taro's version that will be published in a magazine. She and Capa are like twins, intuitively connected, bonded even in what they notice. You cannot help sensing their own story in the two pictures: in photographing this relaxed man and woman, Taro and Capa are capturing themselves at their best. At this moment in time, this moment in history, they are equals, friends, lovers. They are one, united.

BLOOD IN THE BULLRING

Underneath the dream of a new society, there is a dark side to this revolution. Capa and Taro have arrived after the blood is washed away from the streets, after the executions of officers seen as loyal to the army, after the mobs pillage Barcelona and Madrid. Yes, women have been liberated, but they are also protecting themselves, making sure they are not seen as being rich or on the

Capa's and Taro's twin photos of the couple in Barcelona. During this period, you can tell the photographer by the format: His, on the left, taken with a Leica, is a rectangle. Hers, on the right, is a square format from the Reflex-Korelle. Magazines chose to print Taro's shot.

"wrong" side. Wealthy families know enough to put on the costume of the worker to save themselves.

Spain is often called the land of sun and shadow, and that is not just a description of the landscape. The phrase suggests two sides of Spanish history and culture: glory and cruelty. Indeed, the spirit of vengeance runs like a deadly electrical current in divided Spain, sparking the worst in people. In the early days of the military uprising and the revolution, the country erupts with horrific violence.

On the right, the rebels think nothing of murdering those they see as betrayers, as weak, as not fitting their vision of the nation. On August 18, just a month after the rebellion began, the poet and playwright Federico García Lorca was taken by fascists and shot. The poet was known for his sympathy for the Roma (Gypsies) and the poor, and for his homosexuality; he, and anyone like him, is to be wiped out. One of his great poems is a lament on the death of a bullfighter killed in the ring. The last lines of that poem, translated here, could be Lorca's own epitaph:

> *Nobody knows you. No. But I sing of you.*
> *For posterity I sing of your profile and grace.*
> *Of the signal maturity of your understanding.*
> *Of your appetite for death and the taste of its mouth.*
> *Of the sadness of your once valiant gaiety.*
>
> *It will be a long time, if ever, before there is born*
> *an Andalusian so true, so rich in adventure.*
> *I sing of his elegance with words that groan,*
> *and I remember a sad breeze through the olive trees.*

Falangists, who are fascists but do not believe in the restoration of the monarchy, have joined the rebels. The Falangists are fierce fighters, and in Granada their squads drag leftists from their homes at night to shoot them in the cemetery. In the town of Badajoz, American journalist Jay Allen sees two Falangists stop a tall man and "hold him while a third pulled back his shirt, baring his right shoulder. The black and blue marks of a rifle butt could be seen." The man was sent off to a bullring to await his fate. All night Allen sees men, their arms raised as in surrender, being brought to the same spot. At four in the morning, they are herded into the ring and shot. For twelve hours, Allen tells readers in the *Chicago Tribune*, the shooting went on, leaving eighteen hundred people, men and women, executed. Seeing this cold-blooded massacre leaves Allen "sick at heart and in body."

On the left, there are youth gangs who are as deadly as the Falangists. And some of the Left leaders have the icy will of tyrants. They are less interested in

In this 1936 image by an unknown photographer,
Taro is no longer the Parisian sophisticate; her hair, her
overalls, and her look are that of a Spanish revolutionary.

defeating Franco than in pressing forward a total revolution—no matter who or what gets in the way. They are cold, abstract, and unconcerned with the blood price of their dreams. The goal of total revolution means no individual is as important as the final triumph of the people. Anyone may be sacrificed. Because the Catholic Church is seen as a conservative force that oppresses peasants and women, rage has been let loose on its centuries-old churches with their magnificent statues. Thousands of priests, nuns, and devout Catholics are murdered.

Aleksander Szurek, a volunteer for the loyalist side, strolls into a village square, where he sees "a group of peasants burning the broken church altar and holy pictures." He scolds them, saying, "These may be of artistic value. You shouldn't do that." One peasant looks at him "as if to say it was none of my business and quietly threw another piece of the altar on the fire. The others never looked at me, nor did they say a word. I felt their hatred."

The Spain that Capa and Taro are visiting is in a revolution, but how deep is the change? How much are people just surviving, making sure that they don't get picked out, dragged into a prison cell, perhaps even murdered? Is that

Taken in August or September 1936, Capa sees a pensive Taro in the countryside.

daughter of the former factory owner wearing coveralls because she believes in the cause of brotherhood, or because she does not want her family to be singled out? This is what happens in revolutions. Social orders are capsized. But what turns may turn again. No one knows who will win in the end, or what Spain will become.

EL CAMPESINO

After a couple of weeks, Capa and Taro have seen enough of the new society in Barcelona; they are itching to get to some action. They did come to photograph a war, after all.

The conflict is no longer near the city—they hear it has moved north and west. Franco's rebels have succeeded in capturing a good deal of northern Spain, parts of the west, key cities in the south, and the southernmost tip, by Cádiz, along with their original base, Spanish Morocco. A crucial front is in Aragon, a region to the west of Catalonia, which marks the edge of Franco's territory. The government needs to push back in Aragon so that it can weaken the rebels and eventually circle back and protect the capital of Madrid, in the center of the country.

The young photographers find a car that will take them through the Ebro valley. Their driver steers up a long dry channel that follows the Ebro River and leads west from the coast to the front in Aragon. Along the Ebro, the yellow land rises into undulating mountains, some dotted with thick fir trees, cooling streams, and caves; here the ground is rocky and crumbling, choked with scrub brush and pale grasses that scrape and scratch one's knees. Here the skies are wide open, leaving everyone exposed to whatever elements shall rain down.

Here, too, is ancient Spain—farmers shaking grain in a sieve, raking hay onto carts, riding donkeys piled high with bales of straw, using the same tools as their ancestors. Much of Spain is like this: still in the Middle Ages. Vast areas of land are owned by big landowners, often aristocrats whose titles date back hundreds of years. The land is farmed by millions who have barely enough to eat and are no more than serfs. In "this tawny land shaped like a bull's hide stretched to dry in the sun," as Jay Allen has written, olives are grown in ancient gnarled trees and wheat is threshed in tiny villages. Children on the estates are lucky if they have even a year of schooling. They spend their days pulling donkeys through the fields or helping their parents, who barely eke out a living working the crops.

El Campesino: *As framed in this Taro photograph, the farmer is the essence of the Spanish land. He is hardworking and enduring, using ancient tools to harvest the fruits of the earth. This image exists only in a notebook of shots Capa and Taro shared.*

Farmers in the countryside were far from the urban revolution in Barcelona, but Capa and Taro were traveling in Aragon in August, where people who had never owned land were forming collective farms. Photograph by Taro.

This is part of the poignancy and drama of the conflict in Spain: a land where peasants have been farming the same way for centuries is the scene of battle with the world's most advanced guns, tanks, and airplanes. Taro wants readers to feel how naked and exposed the Spaniards are to the weapons of war. She takes a striking picture of one man, an unshaven farmer, *El Campesino*, with his handmade wooden pitchfork against a mottled sky. A hero of the earth and sky—who would doubt whom we must defend?

The photos she and Capa take on the way to the front portray a second kind of workers' paradise—very different from Barcelona with its women in pants and taxicabs sporting anarchist black. In Aragon, many of the large farms have been turned into collectives. The once poor, starving, illiterate peasants have taken over large estates and now collectively own and manage them. During this time seventeen hundred agrarian collectives will be created throughout Spain, involving over three million people. The images of the farmers, working side by side, pitching bales of hay, are also an image of the enduring common people melded with the new, the revolutionary. The collective farm, like the free food in the Hotel Ritz, is the Left's hopeful dream of Spain.

A set of Capa negatives shot in August or September shows Taro playing with a donkey.

WHERE IS THE WAR?

Capa and Taro are frustrated. They came to Aragon to photograph actual combat, but even here there are no battles. Instead there is a stalemate. The loyalist government forces have dug their trenches and pushed their heavy guns and cannons up the rocky hills, but mostly they are waiting. There is so little happening that Taro and Capa ask the soldiers to stage some action, running down the steep, grassy hillside, pretending to shoot at the enemy.

Back in the Barcelona sunshine, the homemade troops, with their haphazard uniforms and their rusty muskets, looked romantic. But the reality of this war is stillness and more stillness, "the mingled boredom and discomfort of stationary warfare," writes George Orwell. Orwell will soon join a POUM unit up in the hills, not far from where Capa and Taro are now traveling. Dug into the earth and mud, hanging on to their positions, and occasionally trading gunfire with the rebels who are hiding up in the high ridges, he and the other soldiers remain stuck doing very little.

Still in search of a real battle, Capa and Taro set out for Madrid.

LATE AUGUST—SEPTEMBER 1936

Sitting in the dry and hot Castilian plains in the center of the country, Madrid is crucial, both symbolically and strategically. As the capital, Madrid represents the center of power. The grand buildings tell the story of the history of Spain as an empire, ruled by monarchy and the Catholic Church. The Prado Museum is filled with treasures and the country's most famous paintings. The city is also key geographically: if Madrid is encircled or captured, the cause of the Republic is almost certainly lost.

In the first weeks of fighting, the rebels have managed to take a chain of cities to the south of Madrid: Seville, Córdoba, and Granada. The government has not been able to make them turn back. Now, with fascist troops pressing in from both the south and the northern hills, Madrid is in grave danger of falling to Franco.

When Taro and Capa arrive in the grand capital, they find a city bracing for an attack. Tunnels have been dug underground. Trenches snake around the city's environs. Barricades made of paving stones line the streets. Militia seen as loyal to Franco are exposed, tried, and sometimes swiftly executed. Everyone is tense, waiting.

Taro uses her camera to focus on the way that civilian life is being transformed. She captures a recruit getting a haircut. A close-up of a war orphan, loyalist cap perched on his head, shows him eyeing her warily as he scoops up a mouthful of soup. Capa takes a fascinating shot of a rebel officer being interrogated. The shot bristles with drama: the skeptical officer on the government side; the rebel commander, still in uniform, arms outstretched, hands open, as if to say, *What, me? I know nothing!* Surrounding them is a crowd of haggard loyalist volunteers, intent, listening closely, some in caps, others in head scarves. A single image tells the story of a country divided, of the fear of spies and betrayal.

For a brief few days, Capa and Taro focus on Toledo, a medieval city south

In the suspicious faces of the soldiers and the puzzled gesture of this captured rebel officer, a photographer, perhaps Chim, caught the mood of anger and mistrust that ran through Spain. A rebel general claimed that four columns of men were advancing on Madrid and a hidden "fifth column" lived in the city, ready to betray its defenders, which is the origin of the expression. No one knew for certain whom they could trust.

of Madrid. There, throngs of journalists and onlookers mill at the base of the Alcázar, a turreted castle that looms over this sunbaked city. Colonel Moscardó, a defiant rebel, has barricaded himself inside the fortress with one thousand troops, local women and children, and about a hundred leftist hostages. "I love Spain and have confidence in General Franco," he declares. "It would be dishonorable to surrender the arms of *caballeros* [knights] to the Red rabble!"

Day after day people wait, but the siege does not end. The rebels and their hostages are surviving in intolerable conditions—lamps made of sardine cans, garbage tossed out of windows, soldiers sick with dysentery, constant shelling

eye; her use of the camera is unafraid, catching a person's direct gaze, like the orphan boy in Madrid who stops midway in eating his soup to look at her. What did he make of the pretty young woman with tousled hair, dressed like a man, who leans forward, peers into her camera, and presses the shutter? People who meet Capa and Taro during the war always speak of her infectious laugh, how lightly she carries herself. For all the destruction she witnesses, she remains high-spirited, playful. "They both had a way of not appearing to take anything seriously," says Herbert Matthews, the *New York Times* reporter.

Clemente Cimorra, a Spanish journalist, notices the couple as they travel across the Córdoba area during this time, and remarks that they are "almost children. Unarmed, with little more in their hands but a camera, watching without the slightest trace of fear the circling of a plane that was dipping in a worrying fashion about their heads."

Capa is also gaining confidence as a photographer. His images are different from Taro's—he likes to whip out his palm-seized Leica and capture the blur of movement, the danger that is close by. They have not found combat, but in their search they have refined their special talent, the way their photos can be more than documents—they can tell stories. Both photographers connect with their subjects, which the person on the other side of the lens can sense. They find the human drama at the center of whatever action is taking place. While Capa and Taro are fiercely loyal to the Left—they will only photograph the government side—in the midst of this war of ideas, of competing ideologies, theirs is a photography of compassion.

Taro and Capa are drawn to children. Her images of orphans eating together and playing are haunting. Both Capa and Taro understand that their worth as photographers depends on their capacity to connect with the people they depict. They are creating photos that are meant to make viewers feel as if they were right there beside the faces in the image.

Capa used any angle he could find to give a sense of action.
Here, in this September 1936 shot, he shows soldiers training.

Capa's advice about how to be a good photographer is simple: "like people and let them know it."

Now, as the couple leaves the terrible scene of refugees, their luck—and their lives—are about to change.

A SOLDIER FALLS

The day, like all late summer days in southern Spain, is warm. The orange sun throws crisp shadows on the ground. Summer's punishing heat has begun to drain from the earth. The fields are sheared, the crops harvested, leaving a bare, open landscape.

The couple has joined a small loyalist unit near the village of Espejo. There, sometime after the siesta period—1:00 to 3:30 PM, when traditionally no fighting takes place—a band of soldiers begins maneuvers on the hillside. Taro and Capa photograph them running across a field, positioning themselves in a gully, and aiming their rifles. The men wear caps with tassels, and cartridge belts are strapped diagonally across their chests. Capa moves in front of the group, sometimes twisting around to get his shot, while Taro brings up the rear. The men run once more up a hill, their commander waving them on, then down again into a gully. At some point, a shot rings out. A tall soldier's arms fly out from his sides; his gun drops from his hand. Capa presses the button on his Leica, capturing the exact moment when a bullet enters the soldier's heart and kills him.

That photograph—*The Falling Soldier*—will become the most famous war photograph in history. It will come to symbolize not just the Spanish Civil War but all war and its terrible human cost. (For the controversy surrounding *The Falling Soldier*, see Appendix A.)

BY LATE SEPTEMBER, Capa and Taro are back in Paris, awaiting new assignments in Spain. That fall there is another big change: the Soviet Union has agreed to send arms to the Spanish government.

The war may be turning.

And Capa is on his way to being famous.

Capa's September 1936 photo, The Falling Soldier, *is one of the most famous ever taken.*

In this Vu cover, Alexander Liberman uses the swastika and Germanic type to echo the mechanical rigidity of the soldiers. The rising clash of Left and Right could be felt throughout Europe, whether in violent demonstrations, hotly contested elections, or actual combat.

CHAPTER FIVE

INTERLUDE:

"THE ARTIST MUST TAKE SIDES"

WHAT IS TRUTH IN WAR? What obligation does a journalist or a photographer have to tell both sides?

In the six weeks that Capa and Taro spend in Spain, they witness a discouraging and lopsided struggle. They return to Toledo, where they watch the Alcázar finally liberated by Franco—a humiliating defeat for the Republic. In fight after fight, the government forces are losing badly. The heroic victories the couple imagine they are about to see are a mirage, never found.

Why do Capa and Taro keep trying to find a government victory? Why do losing battles in a dusty land matter so much? The war in Spain has never been just about Spain. It is about the world. It is about the uneasy balance of powers in Europe and the sense that an ultimate war, a clash of forces on an unimaginable scale, is looming. Capa and Taro know this; that is why they try over and over again to send images back to publications that will tell the government side of the story. For them,

This poster proudly links Franco with Hitler, Mussolini, and Portugal's leader, António de Oliveira Salazar. Precisely because of the close alliance of these leaders, many saw Spain and the defense of the Republic as the battle line between evil and idealism.

twenty-seven countries meet to form the Non-Intervention Committee. The nations agree to stay out of Spain and to monitor any violations of those who might be sending arms or help across the border.

The nonintervention pact is a cruel farce. Anyone with eyes can see that German planes, equipment, and guns are already making their way to Franco's troops as he prepares for a full-on assault of Madrid. Benito Mussolini, the fascist ruler of Italy, does not want to be left out and also wants to test his equipment. He soon joins in the not-so-secret smuggling. Yet no matter what evidence is brought to the Non-Intervention Committee, its members refuse to take notice.

Once the fascists tip their hand, Stalin realizes he cannot wait on the sidelines. He will support the Spanish government—but at a price. What can struggling, divided Spain offer to the Soviets? The gleaming gold and silver from the Aztecs and Inca fill the country's treasury. Mounds of doubloons from Spain's lost empire remain. The Soviets offer to guard Spain's gold from the military rebels.

The Spanish government manages to transport hundreds of bags of gold into a sealed and guarded cave. Then, in late October, over three moonless nights, the gold, now put into crates, is loaded onto freighters that carry the treasure to Russia. In all, the Spanish smuggle over 7,800 boxes carrying 510 tons of gold to Russia. Are the Soviets really going to protect the hoard? Stalin is reported to have joked that the Spanish have as much chance of getting any gold back as a man would have of seeing his "own ears." The gold shipment has become the gold payoff—for arms the Soviets send to Spain.

Capturing Spanish gold is just one way supporting the Republic serves Stalin's ends. The communists came to

power in Russia amid the chaos and death of World War I. The savvy Soviet leader recognizes that soon enough a war is coming in which he is likely to face off with Hitler. Stalin is determined that history will not repeat itself—his government will not fall in wartime. Before the battles begin, he announces that he will purge—arrest, try, convict, and execute—anyone who in "deed or thought, yes, in thought, attacks the unity of the socialist state." No one who is the slightest potential threat to Stalin can be left alive. One by one, the most famous communists are being hauled into court, tortured into false confessions, and led out to death by firing squad.

Everyone can read about the trials in the newspapers. If you believe in Soviet communism, you must convince yourself that the confessions are real, that Stalin is being a harsh doctor cutting out illness in his land, not a paranoid murderer. The more Stalin can be seen as aiding the government in Spain, standing for "the people" against Hitler, against fascism, the more he can convince skeptics to ignore or explain away his own reign of terror. Supporting the fight against Hitler can make even brutal Stalin look good.

The Spanish Civil War is not just a local conflict; it is a "proxy" war with many shadow puppeteers. On the ground, soldiers huddle in their quickly dug trenches; they smoke their rations of cigarettes and idle away their time under the Spanish sun. Elsewhere, many offstage actors are determining their fates. Spain is a staging ground for the future of Europe.

As the Non-Intervention Committee stalls, journalists and photographers recognize that their work is a political weapon. While cautious and calculating leaders refuse to take action, photographers can bring images of the war home to everyone's kitchen table. They must tell the world—in pictures—what is really happening on the bloodstained soil of Spain.

While journalists try to create support for the Republic in their stories and photos, another more direct form of aid is on the way. Young people from many nations are pouring into Spain as volunteer loyalist fighters, nurses, and doctors.

BULLETS AIMED AT HITLER

"Far below and flat to the eye lay Spain," Alvah Bessie writes. "You felt that you were in the presence of Time and Death, the top of the world and the end of it." Bessie, a writer who signed up for the loyalist cause, has said goodbye to his young family in America, taken a ship across the Atlantic Ocean, and then rushed onward to Paris, where he joins other hastily assembled recruits determined to fight fascism.

Once Stalin comes out as openly supporting the Spanish government, the Soviets assign the Communist International, or Comintern—the arm of the Soviet Communist Party that deals with communist parties around the world—to take charge of recruiting and organizing volunteer fighters. Antifascists and communists from more than fifty countries answer the call. All over continental Europe, England, and America, centers are set up where recruits are given money for tickets to travel abroad. Committees spring up almost overnight—Friends of Spain, medical aid committees, committees for Spanish relief. Flyers, posters, pamphlets declare, "Take care! Today it is us. Tomorrow it will be you. . . . Help us." On college campuses, in cities, protests and speeches are given by idealistic young people recruiting volunteers.

And it is working. Starting in October, thousands of young people converge in Paris. They are sent by train to the frontier of France and Spain, where the border is sealed and patrolled by French police. In the dead of night they gather up their rucksacks, their chocolate and cigarettes, their meager belongings, and begin the long, arduous trek by foot across the Pyrenees, the jagged mountains separating the two countries. They trudge for hours and hours, through the underbrush and snow, slipping on wet stone, singing, trying to keep their spirits up. As dawn thins over a valley of close-cropped grass, Bessie and the other volunteers emerge on "lemontrees with their bright lanternlike fruit hanging from their branches." They are greeted by Republican fighters as compatriots and sent onward to Albacete, where they will be trained as soldiers.

Who are these recruits, willing to leave their lives, scramble across rocky slopes under cover of night? Idealists: young people who are desperate— each for his or her own reasons—to take a stand, to fight for a better world. The British poet W. H. Auden, who volunteered in Spain himself, describes the volunteers:

*They clung like burrs to the long
    expresses that lurch
Through the unjust lands, through
    the night, through the alpine tunnel;
They floated over the oceans;
They walked the passes. All presented
    their lives.*

"There has been nothing like the International Column in modern history," writes Herbert Matthews of the

FOR SPAIN

INDIAN EVENING

ARRANGED BY SEHRI SAKLATVALA

Speakers:

JOHN STRACHEY
ISABEL BROWN
INDIRA NEHRU
(Daughter of President Nehru)

MIRA DEVI
Brilliant Classical Dancer from
INDIA

To those in India who were struggling for freedom from British colonialism, the conflict in Spain seemed like one act in a global conflict. This rally in London drew the presence of Jawaharlal Nehru, who became the first prime minister of independent India, and his daughter, Indira, who later followed as prime minister under her married name of Indira Gandhi.

Laughter in Madrid

By Langston Hughes

THE thing about living in Madrid these days is that you never know when a shell is going to fall. Or where. Any time is firing time for Franco. Imagine yourself sitting calmly in the front room when, without the least ... days ago four shells went through the walls of the Hotel Florida,

Langston Hughes's short essay about living in Madrid as it was under assault from Franco features both the difficulties people faced and the good spirits they maintained. Being in Spain as part of an international movement—and away from American racism—was thrilling to him.

New York Times. "I suppose one would have to go back to the Crusades to find a group of men, from all over the known world, fighting purely and simply for an ideal."

Some are Communist Party members who are convinced that Spain is the place to test their dreams. They believe, Bessie writes, "there would someday be a world of people who would see in money no more than a medium of exchange, the fruit of honest labor, not the symbol of superiority, of human bondage." Some are refugees from Hitler's Germany and an increasingly dangerous Europe. "From the first day of the outbreak of the civil war in Spain, . . . I never left the radio and avidly followed the events," Aleksander Szurek explains. "We young communists lived under constant tension ever since Hitler had gained power in Germany three years before."

There are women who are eager to break out of their hemmed-in lives and who work as medics and nurses. There are also the unemployed mechanics and factory workers who see themselves in the faces of Spanish workers and peasants. And there are African Americans, who have experienced prejudice in their homeland and see their own struggle in Spain.

The great African American singer, actor, and social activist Paul Robeson hurries to Spain. He is thrilled at what seems to him the absolute absence of racism and the fearless courage of those he is meeting. Their fight has become his. "We must know," he writes in his notebook, "that Spain is our Front Line." To fight Franco and Hitler in Spain is to stand against racism and lynching in America—the two battles are part of the same war. That realization marks a "major turning point in my life."

Speaking to a large crowd at a London rally—and an even larger international radio audience—Robeson tells the world what Spain means to him: "The artist must take sides. He must elect to fight for freedom or slavery. I have made my choice. I had no alternative. . . . The liberation of Spain from the oppression of fascist reactionaries is not a private matter of the Spaniards, but the common cause of all advanced and progressive humanity."

The poet Langston Hughes shares Robeson's sense of what Spain means. His time in the country has opened his eyes. "I've met wide-awake Negroes," he explains, "from various parts of the world—New York, our Middle West, the French West Indies, Cuba, Africa—some stationed here, others on leave from their battalions—all of them here because they know that if fascism creeps across Spain, across Europe, and then across the world, there will be no more place for intelligent young Negroes at all. In fact, no decent place for any Negroes— because fascism preaches the creed of Nordic supremacy and a world for whites alone." Spain has given Hughes a sense of being part of an international struggle.

Jessica Mitford, who shocked her aristocratic British family when she ran off to Spain to volunteer, explains why she came: "I cut pictures of women guerrillas out of the papers, determined, steady-looking women, wiry, bright-eyed, gaunt-faced, some middle aged, some almost little girls. How to take my place at their side?"

Many of the volunteers are young, so young, in a world that seems to chew them up and spit them into Spain. Here they are, in wool-lined coats and caps, positioned behind sandbags and machine guns, with "an indifference to danger," writes German volunteer Gustav Regler. "Most of them were émigrés who for three years had suffered humiliation at the hands of the Paris, Prague, and Swiss police. . . . The constant threat of death, which they laughed at or at the least ignored, had restored their dignity. Many were Jews, and their bullets in the darkness were aimed at Hitler."

Each volunteer pours his or her own pain and suffering, ideals, and dreams into this conflict. Spain gives hope and meaning to a generation of young people who have seen the breadlines and hunger and desperation, who have run from the ominous shadow of fascism. Fighting for the Spanish government gives them a chance to prove themselves in battle, and to try to make their visions of a better world come true. They can fight evil and build a new future. That is why people arrive representing lands tens of thousands of miles away.

Mulk Raj Anand, a writer active in the fight against British rule in India, also volunteers, and Jawaharlal Nehru, a very close associate of Indian independence leader Gandhi's, visits. To these freedom fighters, Spain is the center of a global struggle against oppression. "In Spain today," Nehru says, "our battles are being fought, and we watch this struggle not merely with the sympathy of friendly outsiders but with the painful anxiety of those who are themselves involved in it."

When recruits arrive in Albacete,

TO-MORROW

DECEMBER, 1936   A NEW SERIES: SPANISH BULLETIN   PRICE ONE PENNY

This British publication was typical of the messages in posters, magazines, and speeches in Europe and America, exhorting all on the left to care about Spain, to get involved, and to realize what might follow if the fascists won.

the center of the International Brigades, they are organized into units, usually according to language or nations. "The

LOS INTERNACIONALES
UNIDOS a los ESPAÑOLES, LUCHAMOS CONTRA el INVASOR
LIT. CROMO MADRID.   SINDICATO DE PROFESIONALES DE LAS BELLAS ARTES U.G

This poster in Spanish announces that the Internationals are
united with the Spaniards to fight against the invaders.

---

flags of Great Britain, France, America, the Soviet Union, Czechoslovakia and Finland, Norway and the Irish Free State, Cuba, Catalonia and Spain,

Sweden and China, hung from the balcony that was crowded with men in uniform, men wearing dazzling white bandages, men on crutches," Bessie writes.

Some of these young people on the left view Spain as a chance to redeem the Communist Party, which has been stained by Stalin's terrible purges. Spain is not just the stand against fascism. It is the pure fight, the fight that can save socialism and its ideals. As German communist Regler would say, "Spain was the threatened friend in 1936 after Russia proved to be the friend fallen into evil ways."

How could they not feel proud of what they had dared to do? Orwell would write of that time as "quite different from anything that had gone before and perhaps from anything that is to come, and they taught me things that I could not have learned in any other way."

For now, there is singing and meeting other young volunteers. There is milling in the courtyard of the training facilities, laughing as they try on too-tight uniforms and grapple with outmoded equipment. There are endless drills on the dusty roads to learn how to handle the rifles and machine guns. There are the skimpy meals served on bare farm tables, the bitter-cold barracks, and nights lying on straw mattresses across the stone floor, men pulling their caps over their ears to keep warm. There are jokes swapped and local wine drunk and precious cigarettes smoked down to the burning stubs.

There are jubilant crowds at railway stops, where banners hang from the rafters, LONG LIVE THE INTERNATIONALS! Peasants raise their fists in salute, press oranges and grapes into the volunteers' hands. And there is the train—lurching forward across the plains of Spain—pulling them closer to war.

Shot in September or October 1936, Chim's photo of the German division of the International Brigades shows soldiers with flowers in their rifles. The unit was named after the head of the German Communist Party, whom Hitler had imprisoned. In the 1960s, antiwar protestors used flowers in contrast with guns— but in Spain, the flowers were a sign of welcome and honor.

In November and December of 1936, Capa was with the International
Brigades in the midst of the room-to-room combat in Madrid. The

CHAPTER SIX

THE SIEGE

OF MADRID

NOVEMBER 1936

REBEL FORCES have reached Madrid.

That is what Capa, anxiously waiting in Paris, hears. After their first trip in Spain, he and Taro have spent several weeks back in France—this time with money in their pockets. In September, *Vu* ran a huge spread of Capa's images from the war, including the one of the soldier being shot. Though their photographs have created quite a stir, and *The Falling Soldier* has earned Capa a name, *Vu* magazine changes direction and fires Vogel. It will no longer focus on Spain. Capa is back to hustling for other assignments in Europe, waiting for a chance to get back to Spain. Chim has remained there, and his photos continue to try to show an upbeat and forward-moving story: a celebration of the nineteenth anniversary of the 1917 Russian Revolution, parades of happy soldiers marching, busy textile factories spinning their spools of thread in Barcelona.

In fact, the war news from Spain has been grim. Franco's troops are

As the fighting raged in University City, Republican soldiers camped out in classrooms and laboratories, surrounded by the equipment left behind.

swinging up from the south and the west, planning a double-pronged attack on Madrid. Most assume the city will fall. The government quietly leaves the capital for Valencia. But loyalist fighters are not ready to give up. The militias, the unions, the civilians—all cooperate to build trenches and barricades, soup kitchens, medical centers. Everyone lies in wait, braced for a terrible battle.

On November 7, mounted rebel troops enter a southern suburb of Madrid, crossing the Manzanares River. The attackers are repelled—just barely. The assault is led by Moroccan soldiers, enlisted by Franco from Spain's North African colony. The Moroccans are known to be well-trained, ferocious, deadly fighters; Spaniards believed they would race into battle with daggers clenched between their teeth. But many of these soldiers are simply young, poor conscripts, lured with promises of fighting the "infidels" and earning money and land in Spain.

The loyalist government forces plan a counterattack, and soon University City, a campus of modern buildings in the northwest corner of the capital, becomes the site of intense and brutal fighting. Madrid appears to be tottering: "The fascists were standing in the suburbs," writes Arturo Barea, who runs the Republic's censor office. "The streets were thronged with people, who, in sheer desperation, went out to meet the enemy at the outskirts of their town. . . . Our ears were forever catching the sound of bombs and mortar explosions, and sometimes we heard the cracking of rifle shots and the rattle of machine guns."

The arrival of the International Brigades—however ill-equipped and unprepared they actually were—was like a scene from a movie. To supporters of the Republic, it felt as if the idealists had come to rescue the embattled heart of Spain.

The next day, November 8, brings a remarkable sight: two thousand soldiers marching down the broad boulevard of the Gran Vía—the International Brigades! Freshly arrived from their secret training in Albacete, and paid for with the new Soviet aid, they come in rippling waves, singing songs, dressed in uniforms with "loose brown Glengarry caps like those of the British tank corps." Geoffrey Cox, a correspondent for London's *News Chronicle*, captures the moment: "They were marching in excellent formation. The tramp, tramp of their boots sounds in perfect unison. Over their shoulders were slung rifles of obviously modern design. Many had scarred tin helmets hanging from their belts. Some were young; others carried themselves like trained, experienced soldiers. . . . The International Column of antifascists had arrived in Madrid. We were watching the first brigade of what was to develop into the most truly international army the world has seen since the Crusades."

These volunteers are swiftly dispatched to aid in the fighting. And it works. Amazed, all the foreign newspapers run headlines, MADRID HOLDS! The poet Pablo Neruda, who is working as the Chilean consul, writes of Madrid:

> *With eyes still wounded by sleep,*
> *with guns and stones, Madrid, newly wounded,*
> *you defended yourself. You ran*
> *through the streets*
> *leaving trails of your holy blood,*
> *rallying and calling with an oceanic voice,*
> *with a face changed forever*
> *by the light of blood, like an avenging*
> *mountain, like a whistling*
> *star of knives.*

Then Franco raises the stakes.

RAIN OF DESTRUCTION

Madrid is on fire.

All through the chilly nights come the whistle and whine of bombs; all night the sky blooms with flames and white glare; all night explosives flash and boom. The fronts of buildings have been sheared off, and residents straggle down the boulevards dragging mattresses and clothing, seeking shelter. On November 15, Franco brings in German planes—Hitler's Condor Legion. Rebel air raids, aided by German aircraft, rain their destruction down on the city.

For Capa, the defense of Madrid is his signal—he must get back to Spain, right away. So he gets an assignment from *Regards*, the same publication that has Chim on salary.

Capa must have been standing right next to this gunner as he aimed through a window slot in Madrid.

This time, Capa is without Taro, who has gone to Italy for a few weeks to meet up with old Leipzig friends. This seemingly small and short separation will have deep repercussions for Capa—and for their relationship. It is a decision Taro will come to regret. Capa will get his first real taste of war. And she will be left behind.

NOVEMBER 18, when Capa sets foot in Madrid, has been a particularly devastating time of bombing and shelling. The day before, Franco and his men sent two thousand bombs an hour whizzing into the city, smashing anything that stood. Capa makes his way through the shattered streets, past the pockets of still-raging fires, and reaches his room at the Hotel Florida. This hotel is where all foreign journalists gather and where writers, many of them famous, mill around, drinking whatever liquor can be found and swapping tips and stories. Once a grand ten-story building with a soaring glass atrium, "now it had a stripped appearance, with its bleak stuffed chairs abandoned in the lobby," writes American radical Josephine Herbst. "There was a lift [elevator], but to save the electricity it didn't run."

Here Capa meets Gustav Regler, a handsome German communist writer who now works for the Soviets in Spain. Regler is immediately drawn to the lively young man with a camera slung around his neck, and brings him to his commander, a Hungarian, General Pavol Lukács, who is in a nearby suburb plotting his next steps. The men pull up in a French car "in a halo of blue smoke, its windshield shattered, mudguards twisted, radiator dented."

When Capa explains that he is a photojournalist for a French leftist magazine and would like a guide to a battle, the irritated General Lukács retorts, "Maybe he'd like me to take him there on horseback, too? Get him out of here! If he persists, he's going to get himself pistol-whipped!"

But Capa does not leave, and so the general gives him a skeptical once-over, asking, "What do you really want?"

"I want to see the enemy," Capa replies.

"We haven't found him yet," Regler admits.

Still suspicious, Lukács draws Regler aside and whispers, "How do we know he isn't a spy?" At which point Capa, who senses that the two men are talking about him, says in Hungarian, "Are you discussing my reliability?" He thrusts his camera toward the general. "Here is my passport. One day I will be among the greats."

And so Capa, the confident charmer, the gambler, finally makes his way to his first real action.

ON THE LEFT BANK of the Manzanares River, the scrub grass is stiff with frost. Capa, Regler, and an officer peer across the water, trying to make out the enemy's position. The three are in the northwest corner of the city, in a group of farm buildings belonging to the agricultural school in University City. Franco's troops have already crossed the river on footbridges, stationed themselves in the School of Architecture, and are now in a large manor, the Palacio de la Moncloa. This stretch of campus is no-man's-land. Somewhere in these abandoned horse stables and granaries, the invisible enemy lies in wait. Capa

Capa took this photo of soldiers shooting through holes in a sandbag barrier from a few paces behind them.

follows the men into rooms fortified with sandbags, then through an old slaughterhouse, where the soldiers tilt their rifles through broken patches in the wall.

A scout arrives to tell them that Moroccans are on the top floor of a barn, shooting through holes in the floor and killing government soldiers. Suddenly a burst of shelling breaks out, and the three men dive to the ground. Bullets whistle and screech overhead. "You've got me trapped by the Moors!" Capa shouts, half-frightened, half-joking to Regler.

When the shooting stops and the three men get up, a shaken Capa asks to pause, having soiled his pants. "My intestines were not so brave as my camera," he jokes.

THE CRUEL SKY

Capa spends the next couple of weeks covering the fighting in University City. He takes moody, smoky shots in old medical school classrooms, where barricades have been constructed out of suitcases and stacks of textbooks. It's as if the battle in University City were a war for knowledge itself: laboratories are described by one reporter as having "delicate scientific instruments crushed under fallen bricks, . . . notebooks and specimens strewn among shattered furniture, microscope slides on broken floors, the splintered glass starred like crazy paving."

The opposing forces were so close that Republican soldiers shot through holes in a wall at enemy forces just on the other side of the plaster.

Capa also provides a glimpse of the boredom and waiting that so characterizes war: men playing cards, writing letters, camping out, and eating in an old physics laboratory. Many of the soldiers are from the International Brigades, and inside the old classrooms, men of all different nationalities break stale bread together, huddle in the chilly outposts, and shout orders in a mix of languages.

As November turns icy cold, and a dirty fog envelops the city, fighting around University City intensifies. House to house, floor to floor, the men clash, battling at times for a full twenty-four hours

Two men rest in what had once been a science lab.

a day. Franco's troops capture more buildings. Government losses are heavy— beloved anarchist leader Buenaventura Durruti, who brought three thousand troops from Aragon, is shot and killed. And yet the rebels do not break through the front lines; the city has not fallen to the fascist assault.

Over the next few weeks, Capa photographs battle scenes and the city of Madrid itself, along with its resident Madrileños. Nightly they huddle, listening to buildings "quiver," watching the electricity blink on and off. Outside the windows covered in blackout curtains come the hiss and boom of explosions and ghoulish shadows cast on the streets and canyons of walls. Flimsy buildings, largely in the poorer areas, collapse like children's toy houses. Never has a city been subjected to such brutal bombing. These bombardments are meant not only to destroy houses but to beat down the spirit of the people in Madrid.

The sky, the terrible and cruel sky, is raining bombs as Franco maintains his

When Capa was not with the soldiers during the November–December fighting in Madrid, he recorded the human consequences of war. Here, a family finds refuge in a subway station.

aerial assault. In Capa's photos, we see so many faces, tipped upward, hearing the low hum of motors, scanning for the telltale signs of airplanes. We see, too, families crouched and huddled on the cold concrete floors of subway stations, where they have fled for shelter, with pots, bottles, and blankets gathered around them. The ground overhead thuds and booms; the children laugh and play. We see the exposed innards of buildings, a lone iron bed frame under a wrecked roof.

Anyone who can be spared from the fighting leaves Madrid. Every day fifteen thousand women and children are evacuated from the city. A proud capital has become an endless caravan of refugees, standing beside their bedding or striding away with several chairs slung over a shoulder.

Capa—along with Chim and eventually Taro—is inventing a new visual language, one that shows what it is to lose everything, to be in flight, to be a refugee.

One day you are eating soup at your table; the next you are dragging a rolled-up mattress and a few belongings down a street, homeless. Capa and the others are drawn to these images, these stories. While Capa photographs destruction in the making, Chim shows where the refugees flee to—a hastily assembled camp in the stony hills of Montjuïc, near Barcelona. There thousands try to continue some semblance of normality. Chim photographs them lovingly: a frightened girl with a satin bow in her hair sits tentatively on her metal bed, a doll on each knee; mothers pin laundry in the warm sun; a young woman pens a letter atop her suitcase.

This is what Capa, Taro, and Chim are too: refugees, exiles, living on their wits, with no real home. Capa does not even have a passport or official papers anymore—he is not Hungarian, not German, not French—just a man with a camera in the midst of a war. That rootless condition is rapidly becoming the condition of thousands in Spain. It's as if these photographs are a warning: millions will be driven from their homes across the whole continent of Europe if the world does not do something now.

This is what war looks like, his photographs seem to say. *This is what happens when we leave Spain to be pummeled by the fascists.*

FRANCO'S AERIAL BOMBING—the worst in the war—does not bring Madrid to its knees. In fact, the bombing only strengthens the citizens' resolve. The photographs that Capa sends back show the dignified way that ordinary Madrileños

While Capa was photographing how bombs turned women and children out of their homes, Chim captured where many of them wound up: in a refugee center outside of Barcelona. Here, a girl holds two dolls whose eyes seem as watchful and concerned as hers.

Capa shows Madrid after the bombing: coming up for air, soldiers emerge from their dugouts.

are coping: lining up to donate blood, making homes in the metro stations. His images broadcast the message that maybe, just maybe, the war might be won by the government. Determination and courage may hold against terror. Like the slogan on banners that hang across the streets of the capital—NO PASARÁN—Franco's men will not pass, will not enter, will not win. Madrileños will not succumb.

Again and again La Pasionaria, the intense Spanish communist orator, uses the radio to exhort the people of Madrid to hold fast. Tiny, angular, with a severe face, wearing widow's black, she visits the soldiers in University City. Over the radio she urges women, "It is better to be the widow of a hero than the wife of a coward."

It is a terrible winter. The defenders of Madrid walk "side by side, arm in arm, with Death," as the Republic's press officer writes. But it is a glorious winter. Despite nightly air raids, fires that rage through working-class neighborhoods, and thirty thousand soldiers dead— fifteen thousand on each side—Franco fails. Madrid stands.

Capa's photos tell the story.

Children play in front of a wall battered and gouged by bullets and shells.

Even in wintry, bombed-out Madrid-under-siege, soldiers find a way to relax.

CAPA'S PHOTOGRAPHS create a sensation back in Paris. *Regards* devotes page after page to his work, with a big banner headline that reads, THE CRUCIFIED CAPITAL: THE PRODIGIOUS PHOTOS OF CAPA, OUR SPECIAL ENVOY TO MADRID. His work is also featured in German and British magazines. Capa is no longer the scruffy Hungarian with a made-up name. He's a celebrity.

Taro returns to Paris to find her boyfriend's photos plastered across all the important magazines. What does she make of Capa's newfound reputation?

On one level, Taro is thrilled. After all, isn't this what they had worked so hard to achieve? All those nights in their bare one-room apartment, where they pored over photos, critiqued and argued over images; where she wrote his

Although this Regards *spread is about the International Brigades, it also proudly announces that the images within were taken by Capa.*

captions and groomed him to present himself to editors; where they plotted and planned and invented new names? They did all that together. Capa is now a well-known photographer who has joined the ranks of professionals, side by side with Chim. His talent is obvious to everyone.

Yet Taro immediately understands, on a deeper level, that she missed her chance. The Capa she helped invent has eclipsed her. She must get back to Spain to make up for lost time, since she has yet to establish herself in photography. For Taro, it is becoming a point of honor and identity to make sure that her byline appears under her pictures. She confesses to her friend Ruth Cerf that she's "insulted" by not having her name in print. Clearly frustration is brewing within her. Perhaps this is why she tells Capa that she needs to receive a credit for her own photos.

Throughout the winter, Taro and Capa bide their time, seeking out the next exciting opportunity. Finally, they get their chance, with a joint assignment in January to go to the coast of Málaga to capture the rising conflict there.

regards

PARAIT LE JEUDI   N° 152   *   10 DECEMBRE 1936

1fr.25

24 pages

LA CAPITALE
CRUCIFIÉE

DES PHOTOS PRODIGIEUSES
de
CAPA
NOTRE ENVOYÉ SPÉCIAL A MADRID

*This Regards cover is devoted to the brutal destruction of
Madrid, as captured by Capa. He has become a star.*

VU

FIN CIVILISATION

Vu's covers experimented with angles and combined pictures to create striking images. This issue on the possible end of civilization could be a film poster or on the jacket of a modern dystopian novel.

CHAPTER SEVEN

INTERLUDE:

ACTION ON THE PAGE

"CAPA CHANGED PHOTOGRAPHY," his friend and a fellow photographer Gisèle Freund would say. "He created a demand for action. He got editors used to photos taken close up to frontline action." Energy, dynamism—still photos that read with the pace of a movie—this is exactly what the magazine editors want.

Life is speeding up—not only through technologies such as cars, airplanes, movies, radios, and telephones, but in the rush of ideas and clash of mass movements. Movie theaters are filled with eager viewers. Before each showing comes a news-reel giving a fast-moving pageant of wars, protests, marching troops, larger-than-life dictators mesmerizing cheering crowds, as well as the latest clips of royalty, movie stars, and sports heroes. Everyone wants action images that bring the world right to them. Just in time for the civil war in Spain, magazine editors have figured out how to make their photo-filled pages as powerful, lively, and direct as a newsreel.

A magazine is a set of blank pages until images and text fill them. Where should the images go? There can be one picture per page, marching through

Alexander Liberman's design captured the electric power of radio to ignore distance and beam stories across the air.

the magazine like fence posts. But why? What if you lay pictures out across two facing pages, called a spread? What if you angle photos from the top of one page to the bottom of the next page, or make one giant image, like a movie close-up, while a sequence of others run next to it like a newsreel? Capa understood what the editors were looking for and how they might use the images he was sending to them.

Capa had an "automatic sense of the proper continuity for a picture story," photographer Cartier-Bresson observes. Photos are no longer illustrations, showing in a picture what a writer describes in words. Now they unfold one after the other as stories— photo essays—guiding the eye across pages, spreads, into the heart of war.

The picture editors have learned from the experimental Russian painters and graphic designers called the constructivists. Those artists saw factories as churches, machines as sculptures, radio towers as the new temples. Straight lines replaced the familiar curves of the human body. To make viewers feel the change, the triumph of the new, constructivists treated images not as static portraits but rather as objects themselves. They would take pictures apart, rearrange them, and put them back together using slanted angles. The new tempo and disruption of modern life broke images apart and splattered them across pages.

Constructivism flourished in the early days of the Russian Revolution, before Stalin decided that workers needed clear portraits of heroic workers. In Hungary, where Capa came from, avant-garde photography was also in vogue, with objects and scenes shot from disorienting angles. In Paris, another artistic movement inspired the editors: cubism. The cubist painters such as Pablo Picasso and Georges Braque realized that there was no point in treating a painting as a fake window that fools your eye into thinking you are seeing a person, a flower, a cat. Photos could do that perfectly well. No, a painting is flat lines on flat paper. Cubists might show one image seen

Capa, Taro, and Chim all kept contact notebooks, where they pasted their prints. They used them to record the shots they had taken and sometimes to show editors potential stories. Chim often rigorously edited his notebooks, taking out the images he did not think were good or relevant.

from many angles at once, emphasizing that you see only two dimensions. They might paint a guitar by layering a drawing on top of a newspaper, creating a collage in which the actual strings and shape of the instrument are barely

UNE FEMM
BALLON, L'I
DU SABLE : E
DE LA MER,
ÉLÉMENTS
CRÉENT TOU
ATMOSPHÈ
GRACE ET DE
PHOTO HUB

VA-
VA-
NO
TO
PH

NE CROIRAIT-ON PAS
QUE CE JEUNE ATHLÈTE
DESCEND, EN LIGNE
DIRECTE, DU CIEL ?...
PHOTO STEINER

C'EST UNE JOIE, ASSU-
RÉMENT, QUE D'ÊTRE PRI-
SONNIÈRE DANS CETTE
SPHÈRE MÉTALLIQUE QUI
ROULE SUR LE SABLE.
PHOTO SCHALL

D'UNE DÉTENTE, CETTE
RIANTE SPORTIVE
VA REJOINDRE L'AZUR.
PHOTO STEINER

La plage est devenue un terrain multisport. Voley-ball, basket-ball, croquet, anneaux, ballon géant, tennis de fantaisie — on s'y adonne à tous les exercices. Gageons que cette année la bicyclette, ressuscitée, connaîtra une grande vogue. Et pourtant la principale occupation de la plupart des estivants est encore de ne rien faire... ou plutôt de laisser le soleil rôtir leur épiderme. La plage, ainsi, est devenue le lieu d'un étonnant contraste. A côté d'un alignement de ventres paresseux et de dos enregistreurs de lumière solaire, on est étourdi par un mouvement perpétuel de gens qui courent, qui luttent, qui rivalisent de force ou d'adresse en poussant de grands cris. Tout un monde inactif est ainsi le témoin d'une foule turbulente, occupée à de multiples tâches sportives, baignant (c'est le cas de le dire) dans cette euphorie incomparable où vous mènent, de concert, mouvements, soleil, ciel bleu, air pur...
Mais le plaisir ne naît-il pas des contrastes ?

N° 484 VU P. 860

Vu *celebrates "the joy of movement" in this June 1937 spread. Motion is everywhere—not in static photos of people at play but in the flow of those images, which takes the eye on a roller-coaster ride, swinging up and back and flipping upside down.*

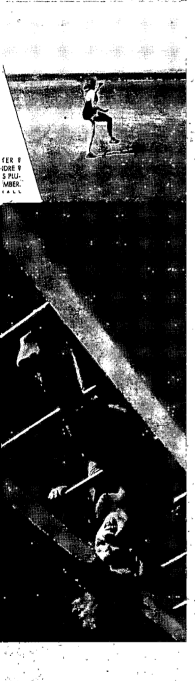

visible. Inspired by these radical artists, magazine editors position photos in jarring juxtapositions. Readers experience both attention-grabbing disruption and an enticing flow of storytelling pictures.

Often a spread will feature large scene-setting photos of, for example, bombed-out buildings. Set in front of the buildings would be images of people, the refugees made homeless by the bombs. The page tells two stories—the physical damage and the human cost. These spreads are dynamic; they leap off the page. And they are hugely popular.

With this spread, Regards *tells the story of a Catholic Mass held in the open air in the Basque region of Spain. The sequence of images is as important as any single shot—making the spread a kind of newsreel. In this region, the church was allied with the Republic, while in the rest of Spain, the church supported the rebels.*

Chim took this picture of a mother nursing her baby while listening to the same 1936 land-reform speech that excited the crowd in the Popular Front image on page 29.

In this new world of photo news magazines, some images are manipulated for effect—and are not exact reporting. Capa's images of refugees fleeing Cerro Muriano are used in a story on Málaga, for instance. The composite images are compiled by the magazine editors, arranged for emotional and aesthetic impact. One of the most famous shots was taken by Chim in the spring of 1936. He captured a crowd staring up at the sky. In the very center is a mother whose baby is nursing at her breast while she squints upward, her face half lit with sunlight. The image was used on the cover of *Madrid*, a leftist publication about the defense of the city. On that cover, the photo of the mother is cropped to show her in the bottom left corner, a huge German bomb with a swastika raining down the right, while a squadron of black airplanes take off against the sky.

In fact, the woman was not looking up at German bombers—she was part of a crowd listening to a land-reform speech and had caught sight of government airplanes. And yet that image of heads craned with worried eyes contrasted against the German bomb and airplanes does speak to real conditions. The Spanish people are living under a vicious aerial bombing. "What was new and prophetic about the war in Spain," the American war correspondent Martha Gellhorn notes, "was the life of the civilians, who stayed at home and had war brought to them." These photographs and layouts are being used to make symbolic points, to get at a deeper truth.

In Europe, people are eager for news that brings them right into the action. So a photo spread by Capa is seen by millions. His celebrity status, his impact as a photographer, is instantaneous. In November, the publisher of *Time* magazine, Henry Luce, begins a new American publication—*Life* magazine—fashioned after *Vu*. The first issue sells nearly half a million copies within hours of being put on the newsstands. The spreads in *Life* magazine do not make use of slanted angles; they tend to display the photos in a more straightforward manner. But the magazine does tell a story in pictures, flowing like a film from page to page.

And the American public is devouring these images just as fast as their European counterparts.

In these few months, the age of modern photojournalism and war

The cover of a publication meant to alert people about the fascist assault on Madrid uses Chim's photo in an arresting collage.

photography is born. Capa and Taro, along with Chim and others, are its creators. They are inventing a form that is utterly new. They are feeding news images that swiftly spread and can have a powerful impact on people all over the world. With this new revolutionary way of seeing, they are doing whatever they can to change hearts and minds. If governments won't listen, they seem to be saying, maybe readers can be persuaded by seeing the story with their own eyes.

This spread shows Capa's shots of the initial stages of the Battle of Teruel and uses juxtaposition to keep the eye moving. Rather than avoid the gutter in the middle of the page, a central image and headline command the center. Looking over the spread, the reader feels the disjunction and motion of fight and flight.

The crowds in the Soviet Union and in Barcelona are linked in this Regards
spread celebrating the twentieth anniversary of the Russian Revolution. The circles
connected by the line itself echo some of the imagery used in Soviet magazines.

CHAPTER EIGHT

TOGETHER IN RUINS

JANUARY—FEBRUARY 1937

"A RACE AGAINST DEATH"

By the time Capa and Taro arrive in Málaga later in February, the worst of the fighting is over. Once again, they've missed the main battle action.

Perched on the Mediterranean and guarded by a medieval castle and fortress, Málaga has endured many an assault. It was one of the last cities in Spain that the Muslim rulers held on to before they were pushed out by the Christian forces in 1492. But the attack in January 1937 is nothing like what Málaga—and the world—has ever seen.

On January 17, Franco's troops begin a two-pronged assault on the city, which easily falls by February 8. There is only one way out—a narrow single-lane road that hugs the bottom of the coastal mountains. Málaga's residents flee in what journalist Claud Cockburn calls "a race against death." Trapped between the thrust of mountains and a steep cliff edge, the frantic refugees are strafed by machine-gun fire from low-flying German and Italian planes.

An ambulance driver describes "seventy miles of people desperate with hunger and exhaustion, and still the streams showed no signs of diminishing. . . . The sides of the road, the rocks, and the shore were dotted with the refugees, pressed down on their faces burrowing into holes. Children lay flat, with one frightened eye turned upwards towards the sky. . . . Huddled groups crouched everywhere, mothers already on the brink of exhaustion, held down their children, pushing them into every cranny and hollow, flattening themselves into the hard earth, while the planes droned nearer."

Capa and Taro make their way up the coast to a shelter in Almería. Though Taro has been away from Spain for a few months, she quickly finds her focus. Inside the crowded rooms, she and Capa move among the squalling children and the stunned families sitting on their rolled-up mattresses, looking dazedly around them. She takes a picture of a sleeping child, half-undressed with legs bandaged, and a man in a beret leaning against a wall, cradling his toddler, whose head is swathed in a stained bandage.

At some point, both Capa and Taro home in on the same woman: a refugee mother who stands, face against one hand, while her children crouch and cling to her apron. A shell-shocked man—her husband, perhaps—rests beside her, staring into air. What a contrast to the couple relaxing in the Barcelona sun that Capa and Taro had each photographed back in August. Here the woman is caught in a moment of grief and shock, trying to be a pillar for her family but unable to make sense of what has just happened or to imagine what may come next. Like Capa's photos from Madrid, these images will be plastered across spreads in publications all over Europe. The photo of the mother and her children appears on the cover of a German magazine and will be reused many times to show the impact of war.

CAPA AND TARO easily find their rhythm once again as partners and as photographers. He is in love with her, and so as his reputation soars, he tries to make

This photo of the same family was taken by Taro and wound up on the cover of a German magazine.

sure that she does not feel she is falling behind. Capa tries to nurture Taro's career by presenting her with two perfect gifts. First, he gives her his Leica camera. This means Taro can give up her Reflex-Korelle and have greater freedom in taking action shots. Capa has begun using a new, even faster 35 mm Contax.

Capa's second gift is a rubber stamp reading REPORTAGE CAPA & TARO. Now the stories they cover together can carry both of their names. Capa may be using his rising fame to give her an opening. Yes, he is the more established

The stamp Capa created, used on the back of a photo of a funeral (see page 161).

photographer, but he sees them as an ongoing couple, a team, and this stamp binds them professionally. If they both shoot the same story, they are collaborating, not competing.

Taro's feelings are probably more complicated. She has the uneasy sense that Capa has surpassed her. At the same time, they *are* good together. How to balance their own individual ambitions with their togetherness?

Capa, Taro, and Chim are not always possessive about receiving name credit for their pictures. They keep notebooks, where they paste the prints, so the editors can get a sense of the stories they are following. But they also know their images will be cut up, used, and reassembled in different ways for magazine spreads. Magazines sometimes give credit; sometimes they don't. As new photographers breaking into the business, Capa and Taro understand that getting credit for a picture is important, for it will help their reputation, which means more assignments and influence with editors. Still, Capa, Taro, and Chim also see themselves as reporters, part of a larger cause—the fight against fascism. They are soldiers in the war of images.

Their partnership is an extension of the world they are in—exiles who must

Taro, with a Leica slung around her neck, can be seen at the edge of this image, taken by Capa in Feburary 1937 at the front line in University City.

rely upon one another to survive, journalists who help each other out in covering war. Similarly, while Capa and Chim are both photographing in Spain, there seems to be little competition between the two men. They are so different temperamentally that respect replaces either ego or envy. The quiet and fastidious Chim is never begrudging or competitive toward his younger, less experienced counterparts. Given the difference in Capa's and Chim's personalities, they each have something to offer in their development as photographers. Capa urges the shy Chim to move closer to the action, whereas Chim teaches Capa to approach his subjects with greater tenderness. All three understand that they are dividing up the story of Spain, offering different angles and approaches. This sense of common purpose was born in those Paris café years, when everyone was hungry and hustling for work, and they knew their survival depended on sharing.

In one sense, all the journalists in Spain are rivals, trying to get the story, the next scoop. But they are also deeply dependent on one another for information. They form a network of like-minded allies. Sometimes they

A battered chair in the glancing February light—Taro's image of abandonment in Madrid's ruins.

need a hand to find cigarettes or to land a spot to flop for a night. Other times they need to ask for crucial names, contacts, information on where the most important battle is being fought. In the midst of war, other journalists are family; everyone is marooned on an island of conflict, surrounded by fast-moving events.

In this atmosphere of camaraderie, Taro is able to be an equal, a partner, another journalist making it up as she goes along. And there is a deeper feeling in Taro, Capa, and Chim—the conviction that they are on the cusp of history, witnessing events that could have immense consequences for the rest of the world. The simmering egos, their hurts and resentments, must be put aside to get this story right.

FEBRUARY 1937, THE SURREAL CITY

"Of all the places to be in the world, Madrid is . . . the hub of the universe," says *New York Times* correspondent Herbert Matthews, "for the immediate fate of this world is being settled right here."

Taro and Capa arrive in Madrid in the third week of February, joining the other journalists who nightly flock to the basement restaurant of the Hotel Gran Vía, with its pink lights, watery soup, beans, and stale bread. Now he is Capa, the seasoned photographer, returning. Eyes twinkling, he loves telling tales of his exploits in University City—with some embellishments. And he's much liked. His resourcefulness, learned during those lean years in Paris when he was constantly hustling for work, is a wonderful trait for a war photographer. When no one has wine or cigarettes, Capa can magically produce them. "He seemed to be able to get almost anything under any circumstances," Gustav Regler will recall.

Taro holds her own next to the gregarious Capa. It does not take long for the two photographers to be seen as a charmed and special couple: "Their faces glowed with their love of danger, the joy of immortal youth. They were dynamic, courageous, perhaps unconsciously so, but firm and irresistible," the poet Rafael Alberti and his wife, María Teresa León, both notice.

Capa and Taro don't linger at the hotel. They are here to get pictures. Immediately Capa introduces Taro to the same sites in University City that he'd photographed in the heat of battle. Now the troops have settled into the weary work of manning a front line. Soldiers are hunkered down in deep trenches, serving as sentries next to walls of stacked sandbags or trying to stay warm in bunkers that look like caves. They huddle under wool blankets; sometimes they

Facades sheared off in the bombings reveal lives left behind—a dining room sideboard, a chair, and a portrait. Early 1937 photo by Capa.

break up the tense waiting by playing a game of tennis on a street. These are not the moody action scenes that Capa captured before but the tired resignation of troops who are in for the long haul.

We can imagine Taro and Capa during this time, roaming the city. She wears her long raincoat, a beret, sometimes stockings and heels. Now, as they go from site to site, she is getting used to the Leica, grasping the tiny device by both hands, learning how to raise it to her eye and shoot, rather than peering down into the viewfinder of the boxlike Reflex-Korelle. Capa and Taro are in sync, sometimes taking shots of the same scene. Her images tend toward artful composition. When they shoot a regiment of troops, she stands farther back so that the men form long diagonal lines, slashing across the scene. Capa moves in closer, crouching on the ground, cutting off legs so the soldiers seem to be marching right toward the viewer.

Do they talk about these choices? Discuss how to shoot a scene? Does Capa give her advice on the Leica? We cannot know. But the paired shots suggest how comfortable they are with each other and with their differences as fellow photographers. We can imagine the reassurance, the sustenance, they each feel knowing the other is capturing the scene before them in a different way, with a distinct style and eye. No one taught them how to shoot as a team. Collaboration, working in tandem, seems to come naturally to them.

Capa records a building shorn of its front, sliced open by repeated bombings.

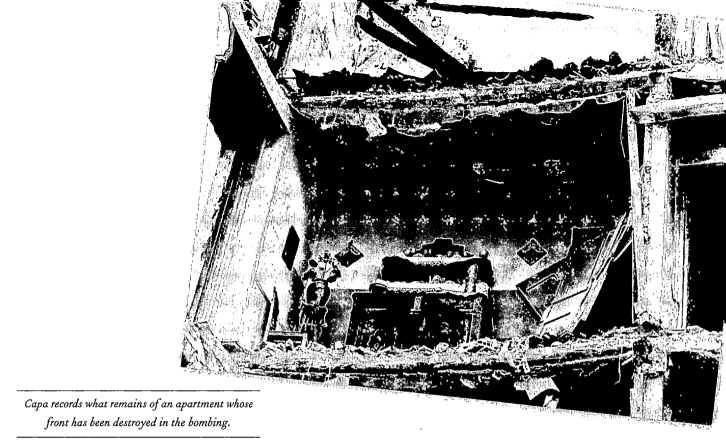

Capa records what remains of an apartment whose front has been destroyed in the bombing.

Under chilly gray skies, they move on, venturing into the ravaged parts of the city, where the bombing has been the worst. These neighborhoods are abandoned, virtually ghost towns. There's a quiet stillness to the work they produce during this time. Their photographs reflect a sense of shock at what they see: a city shorn, emptied out, ruined.

Let's stop here, we can imagine them saying. They are absorbed, picking through the broken rooms, fascinated by a rocking chair left in a corner. It is as if they are all alone in the world, only the two of them, the sound of wind scouring the blasted streets. Shutters bang. Dust floats up from the ground.

Some of their most haunting images are of the buildings themselves, destroyed in air raids: mere facades, windows that open to nothing. Here, both Taro and Capa often crouch on the ground and shoot, as if to reinforce what these bombardments felt like to the residents. A lone telephone pole slants

*Taro frames a shot
with her Leica. This photo,
taken in July 1937, is the
best image of her as
a photographer in action.*

CHAPTER NINE

GERDA
ALONE

MARCH 1937

WHO CAN SAY what happens between a young man and a woman when they are everything to each other—artistic collaborators, lovers, business partners? What is the connection when they push each other to grave risk and yet also try to protect each other from danger? What changes between them when their fortunes start to shift, and they go from being penniless and hungry refugees to increasingly successful photojournalists?

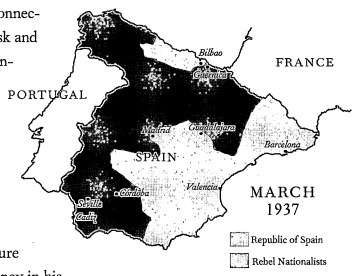

Capa is nothing like the despondent, moody young man who once wrote to Taro from Spain, desperately insecure about his work. Not only does he have money in his pocket, he has newfound confidence. Capa has always had something of the braggart, the gambler, mixed with a rueful self-irony.

Capa rides the swells of emotion, action, impulse. This is partly what makes him such a dynamic photographer: he moves into the scene, clicking away, as if responding by pure instinct to the pulse of action. Taro has always been the steadier, clearer one. "She was more realistic than he and saw things with a cooler head, and thought more than the emotional Capa," Gerda's friend Ruth Cerf would say.

As Capa establishes himself, he sees Taro in his future

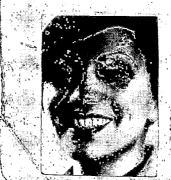

This press pass issued to Taro gave her standing as a professional journalist.

with everything in their life as mingled as the stamp REPORTAGE CAPA & TARO on the backs of their photographs. Taro is his ideal—an equal, determined, sharing the same passions and appetite for adventure and photography.

But what about Taro? While Taro is glad for Capa's success, it seems she may be starting to pull away. Or perhaps she is asserting her independence and sees this as her moment to make her own mark, just as Capa did in his November coverage of Madrid. After all, she is the career girl who wastes no time in getting what she wants.

Now familiar with the Leica, Taro wants to test herself and establish her own name as a photographer. If Capa is a natural at action photography, Taro needs to find her own way, her own style. She settles into the Casa de Alianza de Escritores Antifascistas, the Madrid headquarters of the antifascist writers' union. Once a grand and baronial mansion with a gracious, lush garden, it has been taken over by the government and is now run by a couple who are writers: María Teresa León and her husband, the poet Rafael Alberti. All day long journalists and artists—including the poets Langston Hughes and Pablo Neruda and the American novelist John Dos Passos—wander in and out of the rooms and stage readings. Not only does Taro have a luxurious two-room suite, but the couple lets her set up a little darkroom in the basement. Here, among other foreigners and intellectuals, Taro is at her best.

During this time, Taro begins to tell others that she and Capa are back to being *copains*—companions, buddies, friends. Her choice of words may be not just about Capa but more about herself and her need to be separate, not in the shadow of any man, especially one who is gaining such a reputation. Taro is doing something utterly new—working as a female photographer in a war zone, typically a man's world. She cuts a very unusual figure, and her use of the word

Very few images or negatives of Taro's remain from March 1937.
The last image is of the Arganda Bridge near Guadalajara,
where the Republican army battled Mussolini's Italian soldiers.

copain may simply be a way of drawing a line around herself, declaring herself not "owned" by any man. Or maybe it's a way of flirting with men, hinting that she is available, to get what she needs: a ride to the front or a tip on the site of the next battle. In many ways Capa and Taro are growing up and into their new roles. They were each other's early loves and helped each other to create new identities, but now they are starting to become seasoned professionals. And with that come the inevitable strains.

The young Canadian writer Ted Allan is smitten with Taro, following her around, pleased when she flirts with him. He begins to conjure up the fantasy that they can be together. If Capa is only her *copain*, he thinks, then there's room for him.

Soldiers on the Jarama front eating, taken by Taro in April 1937.

In March, Taro, shooting from a low angle, captures the "general mobilization"
in which recruits look like statues, heroes of the Left. Yet compared to the Nazi soldiers
(as seen on the Vu cover, page 68), they look remarkably disordered and even amateurish.

This may be a misunderstanding on Allan's part. *Copain*, in French, means the person who has your back, whom you can count on within the swirl of a larger group of close comrades. In the atmosphere of the Left, men and women are seeking new kinds of relationships where equality is paramount. Equality between men and women is, after all, one of the great promises of the revolution. Taro, with her bobbed hair, her declaration of independence, is most definitely in the mold of the New Woman. Just as she and Capa reinvented themselves from refugees to photographers with brand-new names, they are also asserting a new kind of modern relationship, one where they depend on each other as equals but can also be free.

Taro plunges herself into shooting photographs, impressing everyone with her daring, determination, and "great courage." Whenever she can wangle a ride in a car she heads out to the front. Her picture of the Arganda Bridge shows the world that loyalist government forces have held the road to Madrid.

Then on March 8, news comes that as many as forty thousand of Mussolini's Italian troops are on the march. The Black Flames, a fierce Italian armored division, breaks through near the city of Guadalajara, about forty miles northeast of the capital. It looks like the rebel troops might succeed in encircling Madrid. Even journalists eager to tell the government's side of the story are worried that this is the end.

"MADRID will be the tomb of fascism!"

This is what the radio blares on the mornings when Taro rises at the Alianza and hustles to join the other journalists and get out to the action in Guadalajara.

The weather has changed suddenly: by late morning a thick, soupy fog descends and icy rain sleets down, turning fields and dirt runways to mud. The fascists, dressed only in light tropical uniforms, are caught unawares. Government planes rumble off the runways and begin bombing the Italians. For the moment, the assault is stalled. Two days later, the Italians advance again, capturing the town of Brihuega. But the government has learned the power of aircraft.

On March 13, government airplanes equipped with machine guns take to the sky, raining fire on the Italian troops, dropping 492 bombs and shooting two hundred thousand bullets at them. "The strafing from machine guns was incessant," writes Herbert Matthews, the *New York Times* correspondent. "Many, many of the soldiers broke and ran under the strain, only to be pursued mercilessly by the aerial machine guns." Some soldiers surrender and flee. In Brihuega there is "nothing more to be seen" but "those two heaps of Italian dead." This is

In this March shot, the New People's Army is taking shape: no more women, or people in civilian clothes. Unity and conformity are the messages being delivered by Taro's carefully composed image.

a decisive defeat for the fascists and a momentary success for the government side, which is sorely in need of a victory.

Taro watches all the bombing runs, clicking away, pressing herself close to the action. She returns at night to Madrid, pale and shaken. "It was terrible," she recounts to the other journalists. "A hand here. A head there. . . . They were so young. Young Italian boys."

Taro has seen her first battle.

THE NEW PEOPLE'S ARMY

Once the conflict in Guadalajara is over, Taro rushes to the bustling government center of Valencia. The light here is strong and bright, and she takes photographs

The steadfast New People's Army in Taro's roll of negatives from March.

of the volunteer army training in a large amphitheater. Without knowing it, Taro is recording the end of the first phase of the revolution in Spain. Just as she had done in Barcelona, she takes pictures of women in coveralls and uniforms, marching in drills. This will be the last time women will be a part of the army, however, for changes are afoot on the government side.

The defeat in Málaga exposed the disorganization of the Republic's troops. Now under pressure from its powerful supporter, the Soviet Union, the government decides to create the New People's Army. The new army is to be organized under the communists, who will provide leadership and discipline. Stalin has his own motivations for demanding that the government create a new military force. He needs to put an end to the experiments in common ownership, such as the collectivized farms and industries. He does not want a revolution. He needs to keep his alliance with France and England, who will tolerate no challenges to private property. So, ironically, the Soviet Union, the center and symbol of communist revolution, has to stop the social revolution that is rolling out in Spain. In the army, in the government, in the cities, and on the farms, the cold-blooded Soviet leader seeks total control. The weak Spanish Republic agrees.

Thus the People's Army is born: a regimented army with a centralized command system. No more loose, democratic units where a volunteer can be a

sergeant one day and an orderly the next; no more long discussions of tactics that can stretch on for hours. And no longer will women be equipped with guns and trained to join in combat. "Discipline, hierarchy, organization" is the motto of the People's Army.

Taro's pictures now feature a different approach, one that could be pulled right from a Soviet poster. The Mediterranean light is well suited to this kind of heroic imagery: in one picture a regiment stands at attention, casting long columns of shadow on the ground. In another, a line of soldiers march, each with a hand on the shoulder in front. One photo shows a huge mass of soldiers in identical uniforms, their hands folded at their backs, standing at attention, listening to their leaders. Taro often shoots from below, so the soldiers become tall,

Taro's photo now graces the cover of Regards. *The reorganized army is finally trained, equipped, and strong—but in the sequence from the smiling lovers Taro captured in Barcelona, through the men and women on page 125, to this masculine cover, there is also evidence of the rise of Soviet discipline over Spanish anarchist and socialist dreams.*

towering stripes against the sky. She is showing order and unity, celebrating the molding of an efficient group. This is a professional army—not the ragged, idealistic individuals she portrayed on the Aragon front. These are images of an army for the masses, aimed to idealize the republican side. This group of pictures is the closest Taro will come to creating pure propaganda.

Taro's photographs will run in *Ce Soir* and in *Regards*—her first published work under her own name. She is making her mark.

PARIS

Back in Paris, Capa waits and waits, impatient to get back to Spain and rejoin Taro. He has settled his arrangement with *Ce Soir*, which gives him a salary and allows him and Taro to sell their images to other publications. He also rents a studio in Montparnasse, at 37 rue Froidevaux. Set back in a quiet street, the studio is

Taro's pictures of the general mobilization receive a full page in Ce Soir.

one large room with high ceilings, soaring windows that look out on a cemetery, and a loft above, reached by spiral stairs. Capa hires his childhood friend Cziki Weisz to print his and Taro's photographs and send them to publications, and he has stationery printed that reads at the top: ATELIER ROBERT CAPA.

But Capa is already restless. For the moment, he cannot get back to Spain. With no papers, he can only travel when he has an official assignment. *Ce Soir* keeps him on less interesting European projects, much to Capa's irritation. It is ironic that he earned the job because of his spectacular coverage in Madrid, but the magazine has yet to send him back. And he wants to be with Taro.

When Taro returns to Paris at the end of March, he is relieved. She, too, is happy, for she is starting to taste her first independent success. Now she can actually see the fruits of her work: her images, some done with Capa, but some on her own and credited to her, are running in *Ce Soir* and other magazines. She is starting to feel more established, if only tentatively.

Sometime in the spring of 1937 Robert Capa asks Gerda Taro to marry him. For the moment, she says no. She can't marry with the war in Spain still on, she replies, as if to imply that her marriage, right now, is to the cause.

Marriage—in a conventional sense—is just not on her mind. What could marriage mean for these two, shuttling between Paris and Spain every few weeks, Capa still without a home country or a proper passport? Even with their successes, they are still refugees in a dangerous world shadowed by rising fascism and the threat of global war. Marriage is simply not possible.

Sure enough, by April it is not love calling, but war in Spain.

CHAPTER TEN

FRACTURES

APRIL—MAY 1937

SPRING RETURNS to Madrid. The city has held, and for now the threat of being encircled by Franco's army has faded. During the warm days, the streets are filled, the cafés noisy and bustling, the evenings cool from the winds that blow in from the nearby mountains. The front is relatively quiet. The International Brigades have had a chance to take a break from their unremitting fight in the Jarama valley.

And finally Capa is back in Spain with Taro.

They join other journalists who daily roam through the same places— the Hotel Florida, which teems with foreign writers "with a fringe of men from the International Brigades"; Gaylord's hotel, where the Russian advisers gather; and the office of the censor. In times of war, censors vet the news pieces that will be sent out to the world. In part, this is for security: to make sure that troop movements and tactics are not broadcast to the enemy. But it

This anti-POUM poster—claiming that "behind the mask," POUM was a front for rabid Nazis—
was published in the Spanish Communist Party newspaper, and then republished in a British anti-Stalinist
journal to show the threat to POUM. The question of who was betraying whom was tearing the Left apart.

is also a way of controlling the story of the war. The Spanish government does not want to advertise the presence of the Soviets, which violates the non-intervention rule. So the censor will not allow reporters to mention the Russian men and weapons. British and American papers are not willing to print stories about interventions on the fascist side—the Germans or Italians in Spain—since supposedly no outside country is involved. All the journalists know they are performing a delicate dance—telling the truth, describing what they witness, but doing it in a way that conforms to the image of those who control the message.

At night journalists and officials eat in the basement restaurant of the Hotel Gran Vía, which is crowded, blue with cigarette smoke, and thick with gossip and intrigue. There is talk of a "fifth column"—a spy network meant to undermine the Republic. As they eat greasy chickpeas, occasional mortar and shells scream and thud outside, reminding them that the front is not so far away. Madrid's current relative safety is tentative, fragile.

Around this time the burly American author Ernest Hemingway arrives at the Hotel Florida. Although he is married, with his wife left fuming in Key West, Florida, his not-so-secret girlfriend, the American writer and journalist Martha Gellhorn, arrives soon after. Hemingway—called Papa by many—is famous for his novels *A Farewell to Arms* and *The Sun Also Rises*, which portray a generation lost, damaged, and made rootless by World War I. He is passionate about Spain and lends an air of celebrity to the cause of the Republic.

Hemingway is the only one who has a two-room suite at the hotel, where he keeps ham, coffee, and bacon locked in his armoire. He's the only one who has a car pull up in front of the lobby every day to speed him off to key sites and important meetings. The tall, blond Gellhorn, glamorous in her slacks and chiffon scarves, creates a stir among the other foreigners. She is trying to find her footing as a journalist in her own right, which isn't easy in this macho atmosphere.

Capa took this picture of Hemingway writing in his room at the Hotel Florida in late 1937.

Hemingway has come to his beloved Spain to make a documentary called *The Spanish Earth*, in the hopes of raising money and support for the cause of the government. He has teamed up with a Dutch communist filmmaker, Joris Ivens, who in turn knows an old Hungarian pal of Capa's: Geza Korvin Karpathi. It is through Karpathi that the two Americans, the Dutch filmmaker, and the photographers meet.

One evening they all go out for a raucous long meal in a restaurant, where they eat ham and chicken and paella, a seafood rice dish. They drink wine and talk. Hemingway is drawn to Capa, taking him under his wing. "I soon adopted him as a father," Capa would say, jokingly. But Hemingway does not like the smart, independent Taro, whom he sees as a dangerous man-killer, a femme fatale.

Hemingway's reaction gives a hint of what it was like for Taro as a female photojournalist during a time of war. For Hemingway, Spain and the war is a man's world. Apparently the American writer doesn't know what to make of the petite, foxlike Taro. She is a multilingual charmer who knows how to flirt so that she picks up tips on impending battles and is whisked to the front lines. There is a halo of glamour and intensity around her, and the Hotel Florida crowd all speak of her determination and courage. She and Capa are partners—equals—which is not at all how Hemingway sees his relationship with Gellhorn. He admires the much younger Gellhorn but views her as a budding talent, a student in training with the master. Hemingway doesn't know how to make sense of the flirtatious, cosmopolitan Taro who is also a serious war journalist as brave as the men.

And that is not all he is unwilling or unable to understand. There are dark shifts taking place in the Spanish Republic, and they put all supporters of the government into an impossible conflict.

TRAITORS

The photographs that Taro took of the People's Army in Valencia, with their message of discipline and unity, also suggest a chilling underside: the slow and systematic elimination of opposing points of view. The cold-blooded, deadly paranoia of Stalin's purge trials has come to Spain.

The Soviet dictator has realized that Spain is a golden opportunity for espionage. Every time his henchmen in Spain execute a citizen of another country for being a "traitor," the Soviets can harvest a passport and send a spy in the dead man's place. Every well-meaning organization aiding the government presents an opportunity to infiltrate more spies, more operatives, more men who are sure to spread whatever line Stalin decrees. Indeed, the New People's Army is filled with official Soviet commissars whose job is to boost morale and to shape the men's minds. But the more the Soviets use Spain for their own ends, the more suspicious the communists become—with deadly results. These dark, treacherous currents lie behind the painful rift between the novelists John Dos Passos and Ernest Hemingway.

Dos Passos has been haunting the Hotel Florida and the Hotel Gran Vía asking too many questions. He lurches around, upset, asking anyone and everyone about José Robles, his friend and translator, who has been arrested and charged with treason. Dos Passos is desperate to find out what happened to him.

Hemingway shrugs off Dos Passos, then turns hostile. He silences any questions about the motives or actions of the Soviets or their henchmen. Maybe, he even suggests, Robles *was* a traitor.

In Hemingway's mind, everyone must be allied with the struggle against fascism. Maybe it is similar to the way he dislikes Taro: he cannot tolerate anything that does not fit with his singular image of solid, manly, unwavering strength. He cannot allow the great sacred cause to come into question. But that does not mean he believes what he says.

In fact, Hemingway is privy to many of the chilling details of Stalin's "justice." His friend Gustav Regler feeds him information about the dark side of the Soviets. The author even interviews an executioner, who admits that there are mistakes. Innocent people are sometimes killed.

Hemingway is a kind of humming paradox. While in Spain, on the front, he only values courage and loyalty to the cause. He can brook no doubt. On the surface he seems to listen to Joris Ivens, who is a die-hard communist and believes this fight is Soviet good versus fascist evil. Internally, though, Hemingway is registering all the misgivings, the betrayals that are taking place around him.

And this contradiction is exposed when Hemingway learns a terrible secret from his friend, the writer Josephine Herbst: the innocent Robles, a mild-mannered university professor, has been executed. It is Hemingway who delivers the tragic news to Dos Passos, who has by now figured out the fate of his

In this dramatic, painterly image, Chim depicts a 1938 revolutionary tribunal in Barcelona.

friend. Dos Passos is devastated, soon hardened toward Hemingway and bitter about the whole cause of the Left, which is about to explode.

BARCELONA

On May 3, in Barcelona, George Orwell is strolling along La Rambla, the main walkway of the city, when he hears several rifle shots. "I turned round and saw some youths, with rifles in their hands and the red-and-black handkerchiefs of the anarchists round their throats, edging up a side street. . . . They were evidently exchanging shots with someone in a tall octagonal tower."

So begins the standoff between the Communist Party and its former allies on the left. Ever since the war began, tension has been rising between the

Communist Party and the other antifascists. The anarchists, socialists, and their allies see the civil war as a chance to remake society and create a real revolution for the worker. "The war and the revolution are inseparable," Orwell believes. This is what Taro and Capa first photographed when they came to Spain, showing the transformed city of Barcelona and the farms in Aragon. But the Communist Party wants nothing of the kind. It will not stand for the rise of rival groups or the spread of utopian experiments. Even as communists and noncommunists fight Franco, they edge toward open war with each other.

The simmering conflict comes to a head in Barcelona. The anti-Soviet groups control a key building in the city: the Telefónica, or telephone exchange. In these early days of landlines, all phone calls are connected through a central spot run by live operators. Whoever holds the exchange can listen in on, connect, or disconnect all the phone calls in that area. The communists set out to capture the Telefónica by sending in an assault group.

The attack is a direct threat to any who are not loyal Communist Party members. Orwell holes up with other members of the anti-Soviet POUM on the roof of the Poliorama, a live theater and movie house that boasts two domes. From there, they can peer down at their former allies turned enemies, who are holed up in the Café Moka and have drawn down the metal grates and made a barricade of chairs and tables.

The standoff lasts for days. Night after night, Orwell is on watch at the top of the Poliorama—rifle across his knees, hungry, exhausted, disgusted by the clash between two parties on the left. "I used to sit on the roof marveling at the folly of it all," he writes. "From the little windows in the observatory you could see for miles around—vista after vista of tall slender buildings, glass domes, and fantastic curly roofs with brilliant green and copper tiles; over to eastward the glittering pale blue sea—the first glimpse of the sea that I had had since coming to Spain. And the whole huge town of a million people was locked in a sort of violent inertia, a nightmare of noise without movement."

But even nightmares end, and the Communist Party, backed by the Soviets, takes the telephone exchange. Soon after, the Communist Party begins an active campaign to discredit the POUM as betrayers of the larger loyalist cause, claiming that they were secretly allied with the fascists. Francisco Largo Caballero, who heads the government in Valencia, is forced to resign, to be replaced by Juan Negrín, who is more clearly under the sway of the communists.

The nasty infighting drains international enthusiasm for fighting fascism in Spain and will splinter the loyalist Left.

Ce soir MADRID 1937...

Ces émouvants documents ont été pris il y a quelques jours. Voici ce qu'en peu de mois la plus inhumaine des guerres a fait de Madrid, une des villes du monde les plus riches en souvenirs

This composite image of the sheared buildings and rubble in Madrid could just as well be seen as a symbol of the fractures in the coalition running the Republic.

PARIS

As enjoyable as it is to hobnob with Hemingway and other luminaries, Capa and Taro know that the real story is in the Basque region, where Franco is starting to turn his attention. Chim has been in the area, photographing an important story: the Basque Catholic Church support of the Republic. In the rest of the country, Franco is closely allied with the Catholic Church. Indeed, many Catholics throughout the world see the conflict in Spain as being between the traditional faithful and atheist radicals. A proud people with a language of their own, the

Basques also possess some of the richest mineral resources in the country. The Basques are fiercely independent, resistant to outside rule, and Chim, through his photographs, is eager to show that the Basques and their churches are not behind Franco's cause. He remains in the area for a long time, traveling among small towns and larger cities.

Since Capa needs papers to travel to Bilbao, the heart of the Basque area, and both he and Taro must pitch the assignments they want to cover, they return to Paris in late April, just before May Day. Paris means a clean bed in the new studio and warm croissants—no longer stolen from a café basket. It means, Regler writes, "long French loaves, mounds of butter, sausages and hams, creamy rounds of Brie, the piles of eggs that were no longer in danger of being shattered by a bomb."

Most of all Paris brings a sense of arrival—for both of them. Throughout April, almost daily, Taro's photos have appeared in the pages of *Ce Soir*—sometimes without a name, or alongside Capa's, but often listed as just hers. Her photos of the New People's Army are on the cover of *Regards* with the bold headline SPAIN FORGES A VICTORY. She too is carving out a reputation; she too is becoming famous.

Yet Spain and the threat of fascism are never far from their minds. Taro's family, back in Germany, has been forced to move into a ghetto, where their house is marked *Juden* (Jewish).

On the morning of April 27, terrible news comes from Spain: the Basque region that Chim so painstakingly covered was attacked—in the most gruesome and deadly fashion.

The day before, in the late afternoon, a German plane dropped six heavy bombs on the small town of Guernica, in the north of Spain. Guernica is considered a sacred city, known for an oak tree that symbolizes freedom for the Basque people. Just as people began to emerge to help the wounded, a squadron of planes appeared and let loose heavier bombs. Residents ran, only to be cut down by machine-gun fire. Like black crows descending from the sky, dive-bombing German attack planes—Junkers—rained down explosives that set off raging fires. Guernica is virtually incinerated to rubble and ash. Over sixteen hundred people are killed while others flee to get out of the way of the advancing rebel troops. The world has never before seen a town ravaged like this from the air.

A few days later the May Day marches in Paris attract over one million people who throng the Place de la République, many carrying banners protesting the carnage in Guernica. Capa and Taro are there, too, he once again crouching, shooting the crowds. The couple pauses at a flower seller, where Taro picks out a bouquet of lilies of the valley and fastens one white flower to her lapel before moving on. In the photo Capa takes of Taro, her spirit seems cheerful and light, far away from the deprivations she's witnessed these past weeks.

The moment is fleeting. Within days, each will leave for Spain on separate assignments. War is calling once more.

He is off to Bilbao, she to Valencia.

This Belgian socialist magazine that had shown the hopeful alliance of the Popular Front also depicts the devastation brought about by the Nazi Condor Legion's assault on the holy city of Guernica. The purpose of the attack was to spread terror in order to punish the Basques and break their will.

CHAPTER ELEVEN

COURAGE

MAY 1937

THE PLANE'S ENGINES ARE HUMMING, its propellers ready to spin. On the Bilbao airport tarmac, as if this were a scene in a spy movie, a dark-haired photographer in a rumpled coat hands a pouch to the pilot, whispering urgently. Journalist Jay Allen watches. Only later does he realize that the photographer is Robert Capa. Already Capa and Taro are legendary to him—their "very simple, moving photographs" in magazines show "the true face of Spain."

Allen and Capa are here to cover the fighting around Bilbao. Guernica was just a beginning. Franco is out to capture the valuable Basque region, which is rich in ore and minerals. Capa plans to battle back by taking photographs. He records a town turned into an inferno when its gas depot is bombed. Ahead of the attack on Bilbao, twenty-two thousand children are evacuated onto huge freighters. Capa portrays the remarkable grace of soldiers and officials as they lead young people up the gangplanks and assist

Usually this is taken to mean that to be a good war photographer, you must be a daredevil, a risk taker, always heading toward danger. Certainly Capa's personality is suited to war photography: he is impulsive and restless, a man of action.

Yet there is another way to look at Capa's courage. As his friend Regler would say, "He was truly brave because he always had to fight his own cowardice. Capa constantly joked about his fear, which was very real to him, and somehow humorous." To Regler, Capa's toughness in Spain was a "magnificent act." Underneath, Capa was "really a very soft man . . . a small beautiful boy whom everybody loved."

Capa himself would describe the "incompatibility of being a reporter and hanging on to a tender soul at the same time."

To get close as a photographer is both to put on the armor of bravery *and* to leave yourself open to feel, to connect, with whomever or whatever you see. A soldier is trained to fight fear to complete his mission and to protect his buddies. A war photographer must fight fear to be a sensitive witness, to bring to the world the human story in front of the lens. The photographer's challenge is to find that balance between the "magnificent act" of bravery and the "softness" within—the tender part of the self that feels urgently for the people being

photographed. Getting *close* is not just
about the action shot—it is about connecting
emotionally, finding the heart of a devastating and violent scene. That is
the calling of the committed photographer.

Once Capa is done shooting in Bilbao, he quickly heads back to Paris.
While there, he ends his contract with *Ce Soir.* The restless photographer who
needs to find his own stories is chafing as a *Ce Soir* employee. He wants to be a
free agent. He and his editors make an agreement that *Ce Soir* will have the
first look at his work.

Then Capa walks into the Paris offices of Henry Luce's Time Inc., which
produces *The March of Time* documentary newsreel series. For years Capa has
been fantasizing about making movies. During his penniless days he would

A soldier pauses near Mount Sollube.

often write his family about becoming a filmmaker. "I want to make movies more than anything else," he announced back then. Now he has the reputation to ask for what he wants. Capa manages to charm the *Time-Life* editor into loaning him an Eyemo movie camera—even though he's inexperienced with one. Better yet, he is told to produce film footage for the documentaries.

Then he's on the first plane he can get back to Spain.

For Capa, life is very clear: There is war. There are pictures. And there is Taro.

BODIES. DEAD BODIES. This is what Taro sees in Valencia. She cannot stop photographing the fallen: terrible phantoms from a nightmare. Cold, pale corpses blotched with dried wounds are laid out on marble slabs, on stretchers, and on the checkered tile floor.

She captures the faces of those who are waiting to see the dead. There they are, hollow-eyed, desperate, pressed against the bars of the gate outside the morgue.

Taro's image of Capa with the Eyemo movie camera. Only a few scraps of his footage have been found.

Valencia is the temporary seat of the government, a haven where many have gone to escape the relentless standoffs and battles elsewhere in Spain. Once a city of four hundred thousand, it has swollen to more than a million. The American journalist Virginia Cowles writes that "people poured through the streets, crowded the squares, clustered in the doorways, thronged the beaches, and flowed endlessly through the markets, to the shops and cafés. Everything was noise and confusion."

Until now, the war has not seemed quite real in Valencia; it was a faraway problem for the people trapped in Madrid. Cowles watched the young men who "seemed to have nothing better to do than stand in the sunshine picking their teeth." Then on May 15, fascist planes flew in from the sea and hammered the port city with bombs. The sense of peace and calm was shattered.

This is Taro's first time living through an attack on a city and photographing

Taro shows the concern on the faces of families waiting grimly outside the morgue in Valencia.

the gruesome, immediate effects. Being under fire is a new kind of baptism into her profession, and it toughens her.

Threading through the stunned crowds, Taro makes her way inside the morgue and then onward to a hospital, where she photographs the wounded. After dispatching her photos, she sends a telegram to Capa, who has not yet left Paris: BRING MOVIE FLOOD LAMPS AND REFLECTOR. INDISPENSABLE. COFFEE CHOCOLATE TOO.

Her request for coffee and chocolate comes with a nice flourish—she says "too" in Spanish, as *también*, not in French. The word is a charming way to remind him of their connection to Spain, and probably the easy way they move in and out of languages, mixing German and French with bits of Spanish. *Oh please*, she seems to say, *give me a taste of Paris here in Spain, where coffee and chocolate are so hard to find.*

Another Taro image from the same sequence is used as a cover photo.

VALENCIA 47036 35 17 1330

JOURNALISTE WINDING APPORTE MARDI MATIN PHOTOS
BOMBARDEMENT STOP TIREZ EXTRADUR KODAK STOP EGALEMENT
WINDING FRONT CORDOBA ADRESSE FROIDEVEAUX STOP
APPORTEZ POUR CINE LAMPES FOTVFLOUT ET REFLECTOR
INDISPENSABLES STOP CAFE CHOCOLAT TAMBIEN - TARO

The telegram Taro sent to Capa from Valencia. The word stop *was
used in telegrams to mark breaks; it was not part of her message.*

By the time Capa and Taro are reunited, the Bilbao that Capa recently left is tottering. Hoping to draw Franco's troops away from Bilbao, the loyalists decide to launch two new offensives. One will be in Huesca, on the Aragon front, where Capa and Taro went when they first came to Spain. Fresh troops, now under the organized and disciplined People's Army that Taro photographed earlier, have been sent up there from Catalonia. The other offensive is toward Segovia, about forty miles north of Madrid. It is being led by a Polish commander who goes by the name General Walter. Taro, who befriended Walter back in Madrid, now asks him if she and Capa can join his unit as they head up to the mountains in the Navacerrada pass.

The general, apparently charmed by the young woman, agrees.

CHAPTER TWELVE

COMRADES IN THE FOREST

LATE MAY—JUNE 1937, SEGOVIA FRONT

THE NAVACERRADA PASS must feel like a cocoon of quiet. In the thickly forested hills, light filters through the pine trees as the soldiers break camp and prepare for the battle ahead. The men saw logs, build platforms, dig out shelters camouflaged with leaves and branches, unspool telephone wire to connect to the lookouts. Their meals are served out of iron skillets on a rough stove; they drink water from the cold, clear streams. Everyone sleeps outside, on ground strewn with pine needles, the sky glittering with stars. Though it is nearly summer, the night air is nippy and cool because they are six thousand miles above sea level.

War brings friendship and alliances; it is stilled time, where you belong solely to a unit—your fellow soldiers become family. Nothing else exists but this: your next task, your next meal, the laughs shared over a wood table.

You get up for more work until the summer light dwindles over the shoulder of the mountain. Sometimes you have enough time to write a letter to a loved one, then tuck it away, hoping it will somehow reach home. You wake up at dawn, dread turning like a rusty screw in your stomach. The time for fighting approaches.

Visiting the camp brings Taro and Capa back to their easy partnership. Their compatibility is obvious to the troop, which takes them in as a beloved part of this family. There is Taro, moving like a fawn in her coveralls, shifting in and out of the dappled light, circling, snapping pictures. And there is Capa, in his long raincoat and beret, the Eyemo movie camera hiked to his shoulder.

Capa always dreamed of making movies, writing to his mother in 1935, "I want to make movies more than anything else."

He is clumsy. This whole film business is new to him, and he probably makes a few jokes. The men like him. He has "a warm voice with a full timbre, rich like a fruit," says his friend Geza Korvin Karpathi.

As Aleksander Szurek, an aide to General Walter, will recall, "We all loved Gerda very much and our General was no exception. He loved everything that was beautiful and good in life. Gerda was petite with the charm and beauty of a child. This little girl was brave and the Division admired her for that."

With the soldiers, the couple finds a familiar balance. Even though Capa and Taro have been traveling on separate assignments, they know how to come together and complement each other as photographers, teammates. While he films, she puts the men at ease. Or Capa sits with the men, talking and joking, while she circles, unobtrusively, catching the soldiers in a moment of relaxation. She takes surprisingly intimate shots of what it feels like to live in a unit on the front.

The ease of her shots is striking—far different from the more composed and heroic shots she took when she and Capa first set out into the Aragon country-side last August—almost a year ago. It is extremely unusual for a woman to gain such access to the front, to a man's world. Of course her access is made easier because she is there with the ever charming Capa. But that is not all. The men admire her for her willingness to be one of the guys. And Capa and Taro's own

Soldiers communicate on a makeshift telephone line.

camaraderie helps them blend in with the men. They learn how to become part of a military unit, just as they learned how to become each other's partner.

On May 31, the push starts. The men march up the ridge, pine needles crunching under their boots, carrying ammunition boxes, rolling cannons up the rocky path. Tanks groan through the clearings, their treads spitting pebbles and dirt.

"You felt that you were taking part in a crusade," Hemingway would write of the battles in Spain. "It was a feeling of consecration to a duty toward all of the oppressed of the world. . . . It gave you a part in something that you could believe in wholly and completely and in which you felt an absolute brotherhood with the others who were engaged in it."

With their equipment finally in place, the loyalists open fire. But the rebels are ready. Almost instantly, fascist planes swarm the skies, firing endlessly on

A soldier prepares for the offensive.

Republican officers consult as they plan their next steps.

the soldiers burrowed in the flanks of the hills. Confusion reigns. When the loyalist planes fly overhead, they accidentally shoot their own troops. There is no breakthrough, only chaos and havoc. A somber procession of stretchers carry the wounded and the dead back down the ridge. Then a retreat. Three thousand will die. The offensive is a failure.

Even as the news for the government side grows grimmer by the day, Taro seems to turn more buoyant. She is a confident photographer now—and more. Increasingly, she seems to see herself as an inspiration, perhaps a lucky charm, for the male troops.

The confusion, the routs, the changed plans, seem not to perturb either Capa or Taro. Szurek notes how they both go as close as they can to the battle. Henri Cartier-Bresson would say of Taro and Capa's relationship, "She was right alongside him in everything."

*In June, Capa (left, in a black beret) sits with men near Córdoba. "Capa was an agreeable man in
a group who did not grumble and used his Hungarian-Jewish humor to cheer people. He had a
character which people immediately liked," said documentary filmmaker Joris Ivens.*

The international troops here are known as the Battalion of 21 Countries. Kantorowicz watches Taro create quite a stir among the unit as "the charming lady reporter" who wore "a beret plopped on her beautiful sandy hair and a dainty revolver belted at her waist."

More men arrive, crowding into the door, smitten with Taro, who is enjoying the attention. And she speaks German! Soon a few bottles are uncorked, and everyone jokes and talks. "You could hear the peals of female laughter all the way out in the fields. It was an exhilarating half hour."

Then they settle down to business: Capa and Taro wish to go to the front line, to shoot the battle that is raging in the valley below. But before they head out, they want the men to stage a battle scene for Capa to film. This is common in moviemaking—staged scenes that simulate the real war. In fact, the battalion won this village back in April, and they will be re-creating what happened. Here again is the blurry line between reporting and propaganda.

The men are excited to make the movie. They push out their chests and mug for the camera. Then Capa directs them to create a battle in which they are under attack. Rifles drawn, the men march and dash along the road, skirting a stone wall, as if evading enemy fire; they run in clusters, across an open courtyard and down an empty, bullet-riddled street. While Capa films, Taro snaps still pictures.

By dawn they are on the real front lines, and the men, Kantorowicz notices, have all spruced themselves up for Taro. "Never had I seen so many well-shaven men here."

Something is changing in Taro. Maybe it is all the attention, the grinning young men, her *copain* and boyfriend by her side. Maybe a line is being crossed within her very being. She is not just bearing witness to *Spain's* war. This is *her* battle, *her* fight. Even as the news of the government side grows worse by the day, she starts to take more chances. During the quiet that settles during siesta hour, she flings her camera over her shoulder and dashes across an open field. She acts as if bullets cannot touch her.

"She confidently believed," Kantorowicz writes, "that her appearance at the front during the fearsome hours of fascist counterattacks would be like a battle standard for our exhausted

This cartoon features the glamorous Taro in the midst of men hurriedly grooming themselves before the filming of the battalion begins.

men. That the charm that emanated from her, her daring, her involvement, would boost their morale and encourage the slender and wavering lines of the International Brigades to make a fresh effort."

La pequeña rubia, the soldiers call her. The little blonde.

"GET OUT"

For the loyalists in Barcelona, the situation is far from charmed.

When George Orwell goes to meet his wife after he is released from a hospital, she jumps up from her chair in the lobby of a hotel and hisses, "Get out!"

Not exactly the hero's welcome he'd expected, having been rushed back from battle when a bullet sliced his throat. But there she is, grabbing him by the arm, insisting, "Get out of here at once."

Barcelona is a city with "a peculiar evil feeling in the air—an atmosphere of suspicion, fear, uncertainty, and veiled hatred," Orwell writes. The communist-led government has outlawed the anti-Stalin POUM, the Workers Party of Marxist Unification. "Even to be known to have served in the POUM militia was vaguely dangerous."

A few days before, on June 16, the police barged into the office of Andrés Nin, the founder of POUM, and dragged him away to a secret prison. There he was tortured into confessing that he was really a spy for the Germans. Rumors bristle. He was killed, some say. He escaped to the fascists, to Germany, others declare.

Soon the authorities, guided by Stalin's communists, are arresting anyone connected with the POUM, turning a hotel into a prison. All the red POUM flags are torn down, its bookstalls stripped. Wandering down La Rambla toward the water, Orwell finds ragged militiamen, still muddy from the front, sleeping on chairs, since they cannot go to their homes, which "had been raided. Any POUM militiaman who returned to Barcelona at this time had the choice of

This shot was taken near La Granjuela, Córdoba Front. This action was a staged re-creation of previous combat.

going straight into hiding or into jail—not a pleasant reception after three or four months in the line."

All through late June the arrests continue as the communists eliminate their rivals or drive them underground. Orwell's own belongings—his diaries and newspaper clippings—have been seized. He tears up the card that shows he's a member of POUM, roams around the streets of Barcelona, unable to sleep at a hotel, where he is likely to be picked up by the police. During his last days in the city, Orwell tries frantically to help his good friend Georges Kopp, his commander in the POUM militia, who has been arrested and is now stuck in prison. "It is a terrible thing to see your friend in jail and to know yourself impotent to help him." Eventually Orwell and his wife are able to escape on a train to France. But they cannot rescue Kopp.

The revolution, the dream of a liberated Spain, may be lost.

regards

NUMÉRO SPÉCIAL

1 fr.50
2. frs BELGES
0.40fr SUISSE
24 pages

Un an de Gue e
ESPAG

Articles de
Margarita NELKEN - Elie FAURE
Nordahl GRIEG - Claude MARTIAL
Robert HONNERT - André WURMSER
etc...; etc.

Photos de Capa-Chim-Taro - Walter
MISE en PAGE de E. PIGNON

Regards devoted a
special issue to the war
in Spain with photos by
Capa, Taro, and Chim.
Taro is now a name in
her own right.

CHAPTER THIRTEEN

TALKING AND DANCING

JULY 1937

JULY 1937 is the month of grand gestures, of conferences, pavilions, speeches. It is nearly one year since the start of the Spanish Civil War. On July 4, famous writers from many different countries descend on Valencia for the second International Congress of Writers in Defense of Culture. They fill the grand town hall, craning to listen from the mezzanine as speakers take the podium. The aim of all the speeches is to support and show unity for the Spanish cause.

Underneath, though, everyone is jittery. The news of Andrés Nin's disappearance has people on edge. The deadly reach of the Soviets is obvious. The French writer André Gide has just published a book about the Soviet Union, criticizing what he has seen of Stalin's rule. The tone of the conference is rancorous, confused: stand with the Republic and its key ally, the Soviet Union? Or speak out against Soviet crimes? The talk churns on. The British poet Stephen Spender calls it a "spoiled children's party."

Guests express solidarity at the writers' conference, but tension over the behavior of the Stalin-led communists is not far below the surface. July 1937 photograph by Taro.

Taro and Capa are circling the conference, seeking the best shots. Even though Taro has been living roughly in the woods, a newsreel captures her gliding down the aisle looking impossibly glamorous, slender, with her bobbed hair, her honey-colored embroidered blouse.

While they are on the sidelines as reporters, they are noticed. The Mexican writer Elena Garro, Octavio Paz's wife, describes them as "wrapped in the tragic, romantic aura of adventurers who were young, beautiful, and very much in love."

Capa is getting ready to return to Paris that afternoon, in order to sell the pictures of the conference and the ones they have taken on the front. Taro will

Ce soir

Le Congrès international des écrivains en Espagne

Devant un passage à niveau fermé, Lapébie, vainqueur d'hier, passe de justesse, suivi de quelques coureurs

VALENCIA MADRID BARCELONA

Don Quixote peers in a window on this poster for the writers' conference, linking the political writers of the moment with the great Spanish literary tradition.

stay behind with the movie camera. Before he leaves, Capa draws aside Ted Allan and says to the eager young man, "I leave Gerda in your charge, Teddie. Take good care of her."

Allan happily agrees. After all, he has a crush on her.

As Capa walks away, does he know Allan is in love with Taro? Perhaps he is counting on it—that way Allan will do everything to protect her.

SOMETHING IS GOING ON.

On July 7, Taro is covering the writers' conference, which has moved to Madrid. Dutifully she takes pictures, politely tucking herself out of the way in the aisles to aim her shots. Famous people march up to the podium. The speeches drone on.

But she's aware of another drama behind the scenes. All day, officials have been jumping up from their seats and flitting out of the room. She tenses; her journalistic instincts grow alert. The government censors are stone-faced, revealing nothing. Everyone knows some kind of military push is going on. During evenings in the basement restaurant of the Hotel Gran Vía, journalists have been talking about the rumors: the government is planning to open a new front. No one will say what it is.

Then a door bursts open.

A trio of soldiers march to the podium, fascist flags pierced on the blade tips of their bayonets. Brunete, a suburb fifteen miles west of Madrid, has been captured by the loyalists!

Taro snaps the shot.

The room explodes with excitement. After the dispiriting failures of Segovia and Huesca, the government decided in secret to attack a poorly held rebel line outside Madrid. The operation was both strategic and symbolic: with the approaching anniversary of the start of the war, they aimed to break apart fascist troops who were in the outskirts of Madrid. The Republic's most experienced and best commanders were sent there, along with eighty thousand men. "There

Republican soldiers have captured the rebels' flag—
and Taro is there to record the triumph.

In these July photographs, Taro records the early optimism of the Republican offensive in Brunete.

were more men, more planes, more guns, than the war had yet seen." It's a grand, huge push.

The day before, at dawn on July 6, one government division drove into the neighboring town of Quijorna while another division launched a surprise attack. By evening they had captured not only Brunete but neighboring villages.

Sniffing a big story, Taro hurries out of the building. The censors refuse to let any journalists enter the battle zone. She will not take no for an answer and manages to wangle a car and driver. Two other journalists squeeze into the backseat of the car, and they're off toward the battle in Brunete.

The day's smoke and gunshots may have subsided, but Taro knows how important it is to show a captured town. There, on a dusty road, she crouches on the ground and shoots the perfect symbolic image: three government soldiers below a sign on a wall announcing the village of Brunete. Another photo shows a soldier painting a Soviet sickle on a wall above the words VIVA RUSSIA. The symbol of the violent right-wing Falangists has been crossed out.

On their way back to Madrid, Taro and the others drive past medics carrying stretchers and the bodies of the dead. Despite these grim scenes, when Taro and the other journalists meet up with a group of international volunteers at the end of the day, the soldiers happily share their rations. As the journalists' car drives off, they hear the voices of the men singing the "Internationale," the

global anthem of socialists and communists. An elated Taro enthusiastically joins in.

Taro has scooped the photographers—she has shown a major loyalist victory. And she's thirsty for more.

WASHINGTON, D.C.

It is July 8, and Gellhorn and Hemingway are heading to the White House, where they are to have dinner with the Roosevelts and present a private screening of *The Spanish Earth*. Gellhorn has a personal friendship with Eleanor Roosevelt, via family connections, and she has long been trying to open the First Lady's eyes to the Spanish situation.

That evening, after eating a runny, thin soup that Hemingway disdains, everyone watches the film. To the visiting couple's delight, the president offers insightful comments, suggesting ways to create a stronger antifascist message. But Roosevelt does not change his political position. The United States will remain uninvolved in Spain.

PARIS

While Taro is streaking ahead of the other journalists to photograph the action in Brunete, Capa is back in Paris. The International Exposition is in full swing. At the exposition each nation has a pavilion displaying its artistic accomplishments and technological prowess. The exposition is a triumph of design. Architects and designers come from all over to see the sleek, modern spaces, the art, the displays of airplanes and inventions. But the exposition also captures the politics of the time.

In the long plaza, on either side of the Eiffel Tower, two buildings face off: the German pavilion, designed by Albert Speer, Hitler's favorite architect, features a tower that resembles a Greek temple, its columns stretched long and tall, its Nazi flags flying crisply. Across the way stands the Soviet pavilion, made of massive slabs and topped by a bronze man and woman clasping a sickle and hammer, a proclamation of the Soviet revolution. This is the architecture of empire, meant to be triumphant, assertive, domineering. Nothing better expresses the state of the world as it hovers between two aggressive, ambitious, and deadly powers.

Dwarfed, and just recently completed, is the modest Spanish pavilion, which was not ready in time for the lavish opening of the exposition in May. The Spanish pavilion is designed to show the horrors of the war alongside the dignity and cultural traditions of the Spanish people, in all of their regional varieties. It's as if the displays are saying, *See what you are destroying by doing nothing? See what we must defend?*

Unlike the other pavilions, which are upbeat celebrations of technology, the main story in the Spanish pavilion is told through photo murals that flow from wall to wall like a film. The giant murals made with photos by Capa, Taro, and Chim have been printed "with a mop on photographic paper spread on the floor," according to renowned photo printer Pierre Gassmann. The pictures are of war,

Taken inside the Spanish pavilion, this photo gives a sense of the power of Picasso's mural.
The sculpture in front is by the American artist Alexander Calder, who supported the Republic.

but they also show the heroics of the Spanish people such as the farmer who now is part of a collective. Once again photographs are being used to promote the cause of the government. The modest architecture of the building, its clean and simple lines, is also a kind of assertion: the quiet strength of a country against these huge, clashing ideologies and belligerent powers.

In his studio in Paris, Pablo Picasso has been furiously painting a mural to commemorate the bombing of Guernica. His tortured images now dominate the pavilion as *Guernica* stretches across a wall and is painted in black, white, and

Chim's portrait of Picasso in his studio, standing in front of Guernica, *his masterful mural.*

gray, like a photograph or an old piece of newspaper. The painting is a scream, a collage of hurt and outrage. Figures twist and cry; a horse brays. Picasso has poured his rage into this work, which is an enduring symbol of antiwar, antifascist protest.

Capa comes to the exposition, but his mind is on another part of the world. Japan—yet another fascist nation—is fighting in China. Capa approaches *Life* magazine for an assignment. Though he doesn't get a firm commitment, he's determined that he and Taro will get on a boat to shoot the next exciting world story. As he sees it, they are now both established photojournalists. He is not as wedded to Spain anymore. He is wedded to their life together, traveling, covering the world's next great drama.

BATTLE OF BRUNETE

Taro is in a very different place—she's sealed into *this* conflict. She's not just an experienced correspondent; she's the one who has scooped them all.

Every day Taro heads to the front, often with Ted Allan in tow, to cover the "terrible battle under a burning July sun." The other residents at the Alianza are amazed at the petite young woman, dressed in her overalls and canvas shoes, who hauls the heavy movie camera and sets off for the dusty, hot village. She will do anything to get there. And her photographs are among her strongest:

Though Capa took this shot in Córdoba in 1936, it shows Taro's almost ecstatic expression
as she crouches next to a soldier under fire. Perhaps this is similar to how she felt in Brunete.

exhausted soldiers resting in the dry scrub grass, soldiers hurrying to carry boxes of supplies, tanks rumbling down the narrow streets of Brunete.

Nights she sits in the Hotel Gran Vía restaurant, huddled with other journalists. Jay Allen spots her "in an alcove in a corner with a crowd of French correspondents. Someone pointed her out and told me what I knew: how she went into the front, into action, advanced with the men to get those astonishing pictures.

Taro records soldiers hurrying to bring supplies and hold the line in the fighting near Brunete.

And how the Republican command valued her presence at the front . . . because when the men saw her—she looked a child although she was twenty-five—they felt that things couldn't be as bad as all that."

On one such evening, July 9, Taro muses to British correspondent Claud Cockburn, "When one isn't in Madrid, one thinks and talks so much about the atmosphere of the place, the nobility of it, the high level of life here, that one begins to have the feeling perhaps one is making it all up, that it is just an affectation. And then as soon as one comes back, one sees that, as a matter of fact, it is all quite true."

A week later, the battle has ground to a standstill. The government troops are short of everything—medical supplies, food, ammunition. The field telephone lines have melted in the scorching heat. Discipline breaks down. The fighting pauses as the government forces decide to regroup.

The lull in action also allows Taro to pause. Her mind turns to Capa, Paris, and the future. She gets a plane ticket to join him in Paris for July 14—another Bastille Day.

PARIS

It is hard to believe that nearly one year ago, the Spanish Civil War broke out. Capa and Taro had little then but their new names, their hope, their brash ambitions. Now they have the careers they want. The newsstands are stuffed with their photographs. On many days, Taro can see her pictures in magazines; she has found her place as a photographer in her own right.

On Bastille Day, the anniversary celebration of the French Revolution, *Regards* runs a special issue on Spain, featuring essays and photos from Capa, Taro, and Chim. *Life* magazine commemorates the anniversary with the headline DEATH IN SPAIN: THE CIVIL WAR HAS TAKEN 500,000 LIVES. Capa's photograph *The Falling Soldier* is featured in a huge spread. The war has changed the three photographers. Yes, they are still young. But they have grown up. They have reputations, a following, stature. They have tried to make the world see as they do.

On July 14 at least a million people

This stamp issued by the Republic commemorates the twentieth anniversary of the Russian Revolution (see page 107). The statue appeared at the Soviet pavilion in Paris. Posters, stamps, banners, mottos—the revolution surrounded you, which could be either inspiring or oppressive, depending on your point of view.

In 1936 Capa recorded Parisians dancing for Bastille Day. A year later, the streets were still festive, but Spain was being torn apart and a larger war seemed ever more likely.

surge into the streets of Paris for the holiday, many of them protesting the situation in Spain. Capa and Taro join another couple, an American journalist who will soon join the Spanish fight and a young Jewish woman from Austria. The two couples dance in a tiny square in the steep, narrow streets of Montmarte, below the towering Sacré Coeur basilica atop the hill.

We can imagine these two, just as we did when they were in the Café du Dome the prior spring, now linking arms in the warm night. Taro is far away from the heat and dust-choked roads of Brunete. She is in the glow of her beauty and youth, her invincibility, the rightness of who she and Capa are at this moment, this time. Her mood is lighter than ever, for she has heard the good news that her family, residing in Yugoslavia, has applied for a visa to Palestine. She and Capa are grabbing life even as they know the danger lurking at the edges. The young Austrian woman whose boyfriend is about to leave to fight in Spain "guessed that Death danced with us . . . but we tried not to think about it."

As their figures melt in and out of the shadows, swapping partners in a traditional square dance, they can probably glimpse the lit-up fountains of the exposition, the German and Soviet pavilions rising like massive white tablets. The smaller, low-lying Spanish pavilion is not visible.

For Capa, Spain is dimming as his sole focus. He is growing more ambitious, concentrating on getting to China, taking the next chance, the next plunge. China is brand-new territory for him and Taro, a chance to take a long sea voyage to another continent on the other side of the world.

Even as Capa plans for the next act in his life, in their lives, Taro can't get Spain out of her mind, nor can she pull herself away from Brunete. She flings herself into this crucial conflict and the loyalist victory she is sure is imminent. This is *hers*. And yet, perhaps because of her attachment to Capa, perhaps because she senses she does indeed need to move on to the next story, the next phase of their life, she agrees to go to China. First, though, she must finish her work in Brunete.

Perhaps she reaches an arm out, leans in close. Just ten days, she tells him, and then she'll be back.

Fifty thousand Republican soldiers were engaged in an effort to split the rebel lines near Brunete, fighting in over one-hundred-degree heat. Taro was stationed by the roadside as tanks rumbled through the area. All of the images from Brunete were taken by Taro during those late-July days.

CHAPTER FOURTEEN

ONE MORE DAY, ONE MORE SHOT

SECOND HALF OF JULY 1937

IN MID-JULY TARO RETURNS to the majestic brick building of the Alianza with its lush and spacious garden. Not far away, in the parched landscape of Brunete, the battle has turned into a standoff that is slowly destroying both sides. Though Franco's forces were initially caught by surprise, by July 18 they have launched a counterattack with a new German aircraft, the Messerschmitt Bf 109. "The fascists brought their airplanes from the northern front to bombard and strafe incessantly. Day and night they had something for us, never letting us sleep or rest," writes Aleksander Szurek. Many gains made by the government are swiftly lost; now the loyalist forces concentrate on digging trenches and trying to hold on.

There are some who believe the Battle of Brunete is turning into a mistake. The government is desperate to achieve one grand victory against the rebels, but the International Brigades, especially, are exhausted. All the

*"We ran in advances where we could see fascists fleeing before us," reported
David McKelvy White, an American volunteer in Brunete.*

volunteers have been sent from one front to another without rest, and now they are entrenched on the blistering-hot plains of Castile, where the temperatures soar well above 100 degrees Fahrenheit.

Taro is like a woman possessed. Determined to capture the story, she rises early at the Alianza and heads out, lugging the heavy movie camera, her tripod pockmarked with bullet holes. She buys flowers for the censor in order to get a ride and access to the front; she pushes and persuades. Her photographs from Brunete are powerful, action-filled. They show the lengths to which she's willing to go to get her shots.

The battle grinds on in the desolate, sun-baked fields. Brunete and its neighbors lie in a flat, dry valley rimmed by blue-tinged hills. The residents and troops on the ground are open targets for aerial bombing by both government and fascist planes. Old churches, family homes, and cobbled streets are being pummeled, crushed to dust. Back and forth, the gains of each side boomerang. One day is good for the loyalists; the next they lose what they've won. Oliver Law, an African American captain in the Abraham Lincoln Brigade, takes command of his men. This is the first time in all of American history that white soldiers have been led by a black officer. But in leading the charge against the rebels on Mosquito Ridge, Law is mortally wounded. (For the controversy over the death of Oliver Law, see Appendix B.)

Taro's grainy image of the damaged church tower in Brunete evokes the heat and dust of the battle.

At night, a gloomy Arturo Barea, who runs the censor office in Madrid, stands on a high floor from which he can see the fighting in the distance. "There, behind the dark, flashing cloud, Brunete was being killed by clanking tanks and screaming bombs: its mud houses crumbled in dust, the mire of its pond spattered, its dry earth plowed up by shells and sown with blood. It seemed to me a symbol of our war: the forlorn village making history by being destroyed in a clash between those who kept all the Brunetes of my country arid, dry, dusty, and poor . . . and the others who dreamed of transforming the dust-gray villages of Castile, of all of Spain, into homesteads of free . . . men."

Taro photographs in the trenches alongside the young men. As David McKelvy White describes, "We saw tough guys crack up and babble like babies, wild-eyed. We saw boys grow to resolute maturity in a day."

Taro seems to have fused with the cause. Like so many of her generation, her background, this is the moment of fight, of sheer survival. Her family is waiting anxiously to see if they will be able to immigrate to Palestine, while the Nazi invasion of Europe seems ever more imminent. Her mother has recently passed away. Taro has nothing to lose. She is driving herself harder and harder each day on one of her most dangerous assignments without Capa by her side.

In the past year, Capa and Taro have learned from each other. They camped

together in Segovia, following a unit. They were each other's second eye, partners. Before, she was the one who carefully framed her shots. Impatient Capa, the daredevil, simply plunged. But in these past few months, left on her own, Taro has developed her own skill at photographing violence and war. Now she, too, goes into the action fearlessly. As the forces battle at Brunete, she is becoming like Capa, rushing into the scene.

One day late in July, she is crouching in a foxhole with the journalist Claud Cockburn as the Messerschmitts let loose their bombs, the ground shuddering around them. They are sure they are going to die.

Suddenly, Taro swivels up and starts shooting pictures of the planes. "If we ever do get out of this," she jokes, "at least we'll have something to show the Non-Intervention Committee." Another time a truck is hit and goes up in flames. Taro rushes toward the truck, even as the smoke and heat blur across her lens.

Taro's photographs are wholly different from any she has taken before: they are eerie, overexposed, shaky, blurred. The artful young woman, who understands fashion and appearance, is gone. She has shed her sense of framing and care. She is all skin and bone, risk and intensity. She is inside the blur of action, shooting like a combatant. There's a bareness to her work now. Click, click—a burning truck. Click—shells raining down on a trench. Point the lens up: click—bombers in the sky.

Taro continues photographing as the battle intensifies with house-to-house fighting, aerial bombardment, and constant artillery strikes.

Taro is there in the trenches alongside the men as they lean into their sandbags and aim their rifles. She jogs along as a wounded man is carried on a stretcher; she's behind a company of soldiers as they surge up a dry, stubbled field, rifles in hand. And she's with them in the small moments of rest—even the man holding a rifle swivels around to grin at her. In that smile perhaps she sees a sign: in this moment they are safe. As she remarks several times to a French journalist, her desire to always be on the front lines is "really the only way to understand and do some good."

And maybe she is right—maybe she is a charm for the troops.

PARIS

In Paris, Capa learns that *Life* magazine has agreed to send them to China. Their

joint reputation helped, but the breakthrough came when Capa explained they would accompany the documentary filmmaker Joris Ivens. He considers racing off to Madrid; instead, he sends a telegram and goes to celebrate with his friends in the bars around Montparnasse.

Back at the Alianza, Taro excitedly tells all her journalist friends that she's going to China. She has just one more day before she packs it all in and heads back to Paris.

Just one more day, she tells herself. And then I will be done.

BATTLE OF BRUNETE

This is the image Ted Allan will always remember of the morning of July 25: Gerda Taro, dressed in overalls, waiting impatiently in front of a car she has commissioned to take them to the front. "I must get some good pictures to take to Paris," she tells him. "If they are still fighting near Brunete it will be my chance to get some action pictures."

The sun is already hot and strong, and it is risky for the two of them to drive to Brunete. The fascists are advancing. Allan does not want to go, but he reluctantly agrees. He promised Capa, after all, to keep an eye on Taro. And Taro has been flirting with him for weeks—he can't refuse her!

"Let's not go too close," Allan begs as they roar down the dusty roads.

"How do you want me to take pictures?" she teases. "Long distance?"

"That's an idea."

She eyes him. "Are you frightened?"

"Yes. Aren't you?"

"Yes," she laughs.

And so they push on, Taro admitting—and shrugging off—fear in words that sound just like Capa's.

When General Walter, tall and imposing, his head shaved because of the sweltering heat, emerges from his makeshift headquarters, he is livid. "Of all the days to come! You must go immediately!" he yells.

In the waves of heat, Taro photographs a bombed supply vehicle as it bursts into flames.

The situation is dangerous and confused: Franco's troops have broken through the lines and recaptured the village. The loyalist units are in the midst of trying to repel them. Journalists are forbidden in the fighting zone. Yet Taro insists—this is her very last day, her very last chance to get pictures. "I'm going to Paris tomorrow," she begs.

"No!" Furious, Walter adds to Allan, "Take her away from here! Go immediately! In five minutes there will be hell."

Allan wants to leave, but Taro refuses. This is the Taro who has grown accustomed to dashing out into the open even as snipers pick out their targets, the Taro who crouches, elated, next to a soldier as shells crash around her, a look of ecstasy on her face. She's caught the adrenaline, the rush, the need to get *one more*.

Suddenly, it's too late: overhead comes the familiar, low buzzing sound of approaching aircraft—the dreaded Messerschmitts—"fast, ugly arrow-heads beating the sky apart with the noise of their motors. . . . They move like mechanized doom."

Taro seizes Allan's arm and they fling themselves into a small foxhole in a nearby trench. "Have you ever been under fire?" she shouts to him. He shakes his head—not like this.

He will never forget that day: the ground explodes with falling bombs. Black clouds billow; clumps of dirt fling up into their mouths. From all sides, they are hammered. Still Taro manages to stand, pulls the movie camera to her eye, and films. After the bombing runs come the gunners, strafing low to the ground. Taro changes to her Leica. She takes "pictures of the dust and white smoke which came from the shells . . . picture after picture." Suddenly a squadron swings straight toward them—they must have seen Taro's camera glinting in the sun. The lead plane fires. Taro calmly keeps shooting.

The assault pounds on and on. Geysers of dirt spurt up from the ground. Men are blown apart just feet from their foxhole. Ahead they can just make out soldiers scrambling up out of their trench and trying to make a run for it.

Taro climbs out, waving her arms, telling the frightened soldiers not to run. Then she leaps back into their foxhole. Finally the shadows of the planes sweep past on the broken earth. The fields grow still. She is out of film now.

Taro and Allan wipe themselves off and stand. Grimy, streaked in dirt and mud, they start walking back along the road toward Villanueva de la Cañada, a village near Brunete. Everywhere is chaos—cars, trucks, soldiers stumbling in different directions, wounded strewn on the ground. This seems to be a retreat, but in the confusion, it's hard to know what's going on. They hitch a ride on top of a tank and make their way to the first-aid post in the village. Once there, they spot General Walter's big black car and hail it, hoping for a lift part of the way back to Madrid.

Inside, though, are wounded men stretched out on the backseat. "*Salud,*" Taro greets everyone and hands her cameras into the car, then hops on the running board, with Allan doing the same behind her. As the car speeds off, she cares more about the cameras than she does her own safety. "Tonight we'll have a farewell party in Madrid," she shouts to Allan. "I've bought some champagne."

All of a sudden German planes appear like a swarm of black crows on the horizon. The driver clutches his wheel and shrinks down in his seat, unable to see. Out of nowhere, a loyalist tank swerves toward them, swiping the general's car. Allan is flung into the air, landing in a ditch. He goes numb.

And Gerda—lightweight, petite Gerda—is knocked off the car to the ground. An instant later, the tank roars forward. Her torso is crushed under its metal treads.

Taro keeps shooting, even in total chaos.

THE DOCTORS TRY THEIR BEST. They take her to a field hospital in El Escorial, a nearby village, where she is given a blood transfusion. A doctor operates on her, without anesthesia, as there was none, and the whole time she clenches down on a cigarette for the unbearable pain. But it is hopeless; they cannot help her. Her insides have been torn irreparably. Gerda keeps asking, "Did someone take care of my cameras? Please. They're brand new." A nurse hovers, tries to keep her comfortable. All night the wounded are being brought in.

Drugged with morphine, Gerda closes her eyes and eases into death.

PARIS

The morning of July 27, Capa wakes early—unusual for him. He is anxious. Gerda has not returned nor wired. He tried to reach her at the Alianza the night before; no answer. Now he grabs a copy of *l'Humanité*, the Communist Party paper, but he does not read it, for he has an appointment at the dentist.

Walking briskly, the newspaper tucked under his arm, he passes trees flush with summer green. It is in the waiting room that he reads the news on page three: A FRENCH JOURNALIST, MLLE. TAROT IS REPORTED TO HAVE BEEN KILLED IN THE COURSE OF A BATTLE, NEAR BRUNETE. He runs back to the apartment and finally reaches his editor at *Ce Soir*. It's true, the editor tells him. Gerda has been killed. Overcome, Capa collapses.

His friends bring him sandwiches and fruit and try to comfort him, but Capa is inconsolable, wild with sorrow.

Nº 047909

108

Timbre à date

EAJ/CSS

7 MADRID 64 30 1600

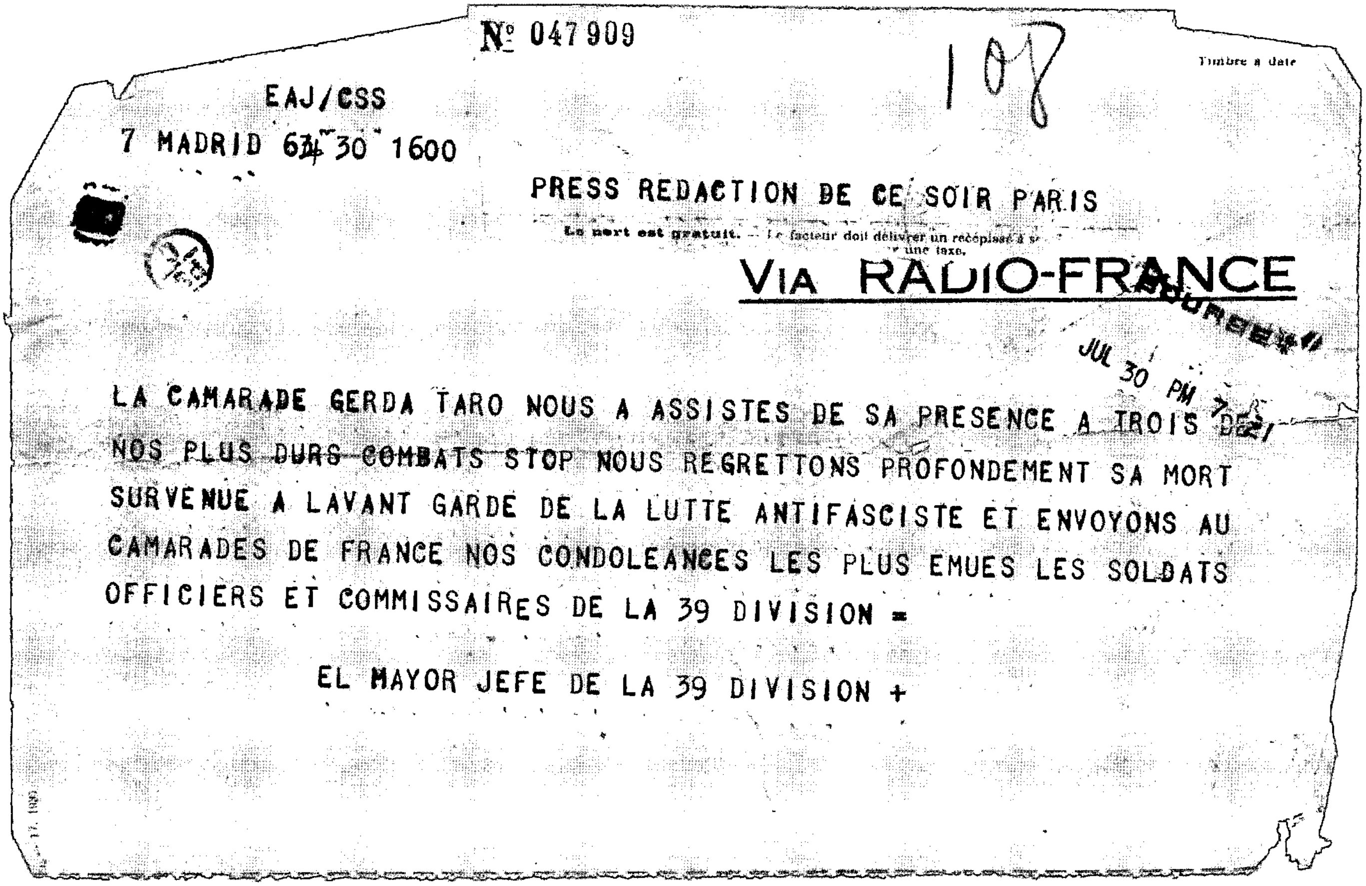

PRESS REDACTION DE CE SOIR PARIS

Le port est gratuit. — Le facteur doit délivrer un récépissé ... une taxe.

VIA RADIO-FRANCE

JUL 30 PM 7 21

LA CAMARADE GERDA TARO NOUS A ASSISTES DE SA PRESENCE A TROIS DE NOS PLUS DURS COMBATS STOP NOUS REGRETTONS PROFONDEMENT SA MORT SURVENUE A LAVANT GARDE DE LA LUTTE ANTIFASCISTE ET ENVOYONS AU CAMARADES DE FRANCE NOS CONDOLEANCES LES PLUS EMUES LES SOLDATS OFFICIERS ET COMMISSAIRES DE LA 39 DIVISION =

EL MAYOR JEFE DE LA 39 DIVISION +

Taro's death is announced to the world.

This 1936 photo by Capa is posed—Taro is the woman leaning on the grave. It is not about Taro's death, but it is often used to mark the event.

CHAPTER FIFTEEN

A MARTYR
IS BORN

LATE JULY—AUGUST 1937

WHEN THE COFFIN is set down on the cold concrete floor of the Gare d'Austerlitz, a train station in Paris, one hundred people are there to meet it. Ruth Cerf and others must hold Capa up—he can barely walk. He is drawn, pale. Taro's father and brother are there, newly arrived from Yugoslavia. The grief-stricken father leans on Cerf until he sees the coffin, when he flings his arms around the edges and starts to chant the Jewish prayer for the dead, the kaddish. Hearing this, Capa breaks down.

Suddenly Taro's brother swerves around, mad with fury at Capa. He starts to shout that it is all Capa's fault that his sister is dead. After all, he introduced her to photography; he took her to Spain! Then the brother swings, slugging Capa in the face. Capa does not fight back. He just submits to the beating. He, too, believes that her death his fault; he is eaten up with guilt.

But there is no room for private grieving.

Taro's funeral has become a public spectacle. Already at the Alianza in Madrid her coffin was displayed so that artists, journalists, and soldiers could honor her. Then it was sent off by a guard of honor to Valencia, where there was another viewing, the coffin covered in flowers. Constancia de la Mora, the censor for whom Taro had once left flowers, recalls, "I could not forget Gerda Taro, so young and charming, with her sweet smile and almost childish figure and face."

Taro has been turned into Joan of Arc, a martyr to the Popular Front and the Left. Already *Ce Soir* has run an issue filled with tributes to Taro, along with her and Capa's photos. *Life* magazine will run a spread titled THE SPANISH WAR KILLS ITS FIRST WOMAN PHOTOGRAPHER, and soon other magazines all over Europe will cover her death.

Now Taro fully belongs to the cause. Her coffin stands in the Maison de la Culture, its facade hung with black crepe, while famous people from all over come and pay their respects. More homages pour in—from Ted Allan, from commanders who had met Taro, and other journalists, filling the pages of newspapers. They write of how young she was, how brave she was at the front. The soldiers who knew her have taken her death hard. One of her colleagues says her courage was that of three men. Her legend grows.

On August 1, Taro's twenty-seventh birthday, as Chopin's funeral march is played over loudspeakers, tens of thousands surge into the streets for the procession, heading through the Place de la République—where they had so often gone for other mass demonstrations—to the Père Lachaise Cemetery. The whole way, Capa weeps. "He was just a great boy, crazy with courage and overflowing with life," the editor at *Ce Soir* said. "Now war had murdered his youth."

CAPA RETURNS TO THE STUDIO, locks himself inside, and drinks for days. A startled Gustav Regler one day spies Capa in the street and is shocked. "It was

Ce soir

Ce que GERDA TARO a vu la veille de sa mort

Il y a 15 jours, notre chère petite Gerda TARO tombait, mortellement blessée... Sur son lit d'hôpital, quelques heures avant de mourir, elle avait demandé d'une voix étranglée : « Et mon appareil ? » — « Brisé », lui dit-on. Elle avait eu alors cette réponse stoïque : « C'est la guerre. » Ses amis d'Espagne ont retrouvé le dernier film qu'elle avait fait. Ils nous l'ont adressé. C'était pendant l'ultime bataille dans Brunete que les gouvernementaux défendaient avec acharnement. Le village n'était plus qu'un monceau de ruines. Les obus tombaient, les mitrailleuses crépitaient... Bravant le danger, Gerda TARO continuait de prendre ces documents...

A card depicts the scene of Taro's death. She was instantly a heroine and martyr to the Left.

the middle of the day, and Capa was drunk, standing on the pavement, swaying." Capa even talks about giving up photography.

His friends plead with him, but he is racked with guilt, pain, and grief. "I left her in danger—she would never have died if I'd been there," Capa would say. "As long as she was with me, she was safe. As long as I was there, she'd do what I did. I would never have let her stand on the running board. That was a reckless thing to do. I would have never allowed it."

Is there truth in what Capa says? In a collaboration such as theirs, what happened when the two were apart? How much did they need each other; how much were they separate? On her own in Brunete, had Taro lost some of her balance?

Had she deprived herself of the way they complemented each other, kept each other safe?

Partnership can temper the excesses of each individual. Capa's irresponsibility, his gambling, was curbed by the forceful and disciplined Taro. But her drive, her ambition and single-mindedness, could blind her to danger. The youthful invincibility she must have felt, dancing in Paris near the Sacré Coeur, may have blurred her judgment. She had started to believe her own myth: *la pequeña rubia*.

Those long days, camping out, bearing some of the same conditions as the soldiers, you start to feel you must be one of them. Living with the men is a way of saying, *Trust me. Let me into your lives. I am one of you. Let me come in close, because I am willing to risk as you do.*

And yet you are not the same. This is the journalist's guilt: after a long day on the battlefield, you can leave the wounded and the dead behind, return to the Alianza, clean up, and soak in a bath. Sharing every day with soldiers, some of them heartbreakingly young, who willingly run up hills, facing a deadly spray of machine-gun fire—how could you not be affected? Your sense of safety, of limits, starts to shift. Day in and day out, you are watching soldiers sacrifice themselves, giving their youth to the deadly machines of war.

As Hemingway writes of the war in Spain, "You learned the dry-mouthed, fear-purged, purging ecstasy of battle, and you fought that summer and that fall for all the poor in the world, against all tyranny, for all the things that you believed and for the new world you had been educated into."

"It doesn't seem fair that I'm still alive," Taro had remarked one evening after a long day photographing the conflict in Brunete.

Weeks after Taro's death, Capa emerges a changed man. "Part of Capa died with Gerda," a childhood friend says. "She was his true soul mate."

"When she died," his friend Cartier-Bresson says, "he drew a curtain on himself."

CHAPTER SIXTEEN

FLIGHT

AUGUST 1937—OCTOBER 1939

TIME SWIRLS. The war grinds on, though it is becoming increasingly obvious that the loyalist army, for all its hope and ideal-ism, is simply no match for the professional forces of the rebels fortified by Hitler's and Mussolini's air power.

By late 1937, Capa recovers enough to go back to Spain, where he heads to the mountain city of Teruel with the journalist Herbert Matthews and covers a major battle. The civil war has fallen into the same pattern: an initial success for the government forces as they surge forward and capture enemy territory.

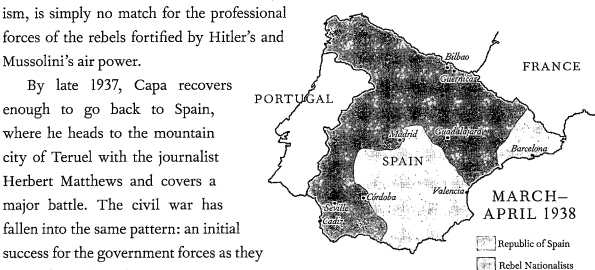

FRANCE

PORTUGAL

Bilbao
Guernica

Madrid *Guadalajara*

Barcelona

SPAIN

Valencia

Córdoba

Seville

Cadiz

MARCH—
APRIL 1938

Republic of Spain

Rebel Nationalists

This book was designed by Capa's former mentor André Kertész, with text by journalist Jay Allen, whom Capa had met in Bilbao.

The journalists rush in to portray a loyalist success, only to find days, weeks later how fragile and temporary the victory. A debilitating stalemate follows, until the inevitable counterattack by Franco's troops. Finally, the government side retreats.

Capa has grown cynical about the war. This is the new Capa: more restless than ever, always moving, careless about appointments, showing up late—as if to assert that no one can ever claim him again. As his biographer Richard Whelan understood, "His closest friends sensed another side of him, the part that remained André Friedmann, who had been deeply wounded by Gerda's death and remained profoundly grieved."

Martha Gellhorn will fictionalize Capa in a short story, describing how he "came and went as he chose, obeyed no one, made and spent money like water, and any man would envy his looks. . . . He made no plans, he roamed. He roamed all day and most of the night, finding people he knew, collecting strangers, eating when hungry, drinking everywhere, talking, talking."

Capa's friendships still run deep, though. Back in Paris in August, when a nervous Ted Allan shows up on crutches at his studio door and confesses, "I loved her!" Capa's response is to laugh and say, "How could you not help loving her?" Then he takes in the bewildered young man and travels with him to

America. There he reunites with his mother, who has safely settled in New York City. He also makes arrangements to publish a photography book with his, Taro's, and Chim's images, *Death in the Making*, which he dedicates to Gerda Taro, "who spent one year at the Spanish front, and who stayed on."

But then he is on the move again. He is finally on a ship to China, now serving as a cameraman with his friend Joris Ivens, who is making a documentary. In China, he shows pictures of Taro and tells everyone she was his wife. In the future, he will have a great many romances, many affairs, but he will never again form an attachment like the one he had with Taro.

FOR GERDA TARO,

WHO SPENT ONE YEAR AT THE SPANISH FRONT,

AND WHO STAYED ON.

Madrid, December, 1937.   R.C.

Capa is now entirely a nomad. He will always keep moving. His only bride is photography.

1938

Europe is becoming ever more dangerous. By the time Capa returns from China on September 22, the Nazis have marched into Austria to cheering crowds and annexed the country. British Prime Minister Neville Chamberlain signs the Munich Agreement in September, hoping to appease Hitler by giving him Czechoslovakia. Stalin shifts his calculations and starts to make overtures to Hitler. "Here the moral[e] is bad, and I don't know what is coming," Capa writes his mother.

Capa goes back to Spain for yet another sad moment. Juan Negrín, the Republic's prime minister, made a desperate move: he promised to send all the foreign recruits—the entirety of the International Brigades—back to their homes. He hopes—really only wishes—that if the loyalists send their foreign fighters away, the world will make sure that Germany and Italy are kept out of Spain. Capa will be there to photograph the ceremony as the volunteers are dismissed. The loyalist side is even weaker, and no one stirs against Franco's allies.

On October 25, Capa and Chim drive out to the small village of Les Masies, where government and military leaders are bidding farewell to a large group of brigadiers from all over the world.

Hundreds and hundreds of men crowd into the courtyard of the Villa Engracia, where they are praised by the prime minster, who tells the volunteers they did not fight in vain. Capa moves around, sometimes on the second floor, which has an open terrace, sometimes down below among the men. He takes some of his best and most moving photos of these battle-worn soldiers: one man,

*Capa conveys the emotional heartbreak
as the International Brigades are disbanded
at Les Masies on October 25, 1937.*

head tilted, his bent arm in the Popular Front salute, with his fist on his forehead, a tear coursing down his sunburned cheek. Another stands erect, jaw clenched. His burning eyes bear straight ahead; he is barely able to hold in his emotions.

In these photos Capa seems to be saying good-bye to his own youth, to the dream of Spain—and to Taro, who gave her life for that dream.

"THE GREATEST WAR-PHOTOGRAPHER IN THE WORLD"

Capa keeps moving. The American press names him "one of the world's best news photographers." Even as the war depresses him, be remains committed to its coverage. And so he is there, in November, for part of the battle of Ebro, traveling with Hemingway and the journalist Herbert Matthews.

Milt Wolff, center, and the Abraham Lincoln Brigade march outside Barcelona on October 16, after hearing La Pasionaria bid them farewell. Photograph by Capa.

On November 7, he steals across the Ebro River on a cold autumn night. Loyalist forces head across the Segre, a tributary of the Ebro. It is a bloody fight—twenty-five thousand will be killed on the loyalist side, soldiers desperately digging into the jagged, rocky outcrops. The battle leaves behind a haunted landscape, with cartridges littering the broken, dry ground and villages abandoned as ghost towns. So many die there and lie unburied, unremembered, entombed in the ruins.

The whole of Capa, every fiber in his body, lives for action—the next shot, the next assignment—and the comradeship of those he meets on the road. He pushes himself, even as he knows the situation in Spain is dire, nearly hopeless, even as he is on the brink of exhaustion. His photos of this battle are lauded everywhere: THE GREATEST WAR-PHOTOGRAPHER IN THE WORLD: ROBERT CAPA, England's new *Picture Post* declares, devoting eleven pages to his work along with a big image of him. LIFE'S CAMERA GETS CLOSER TO SPANISH WAR THAN ANY CAMERA HAS EVER GOT BEFORE, announces the American photo magazine in December. Capa's work in *Picture Post* is his richest to date, and since he writes the text and captions to accompany the photographs, it also offers us a rare glimpse into his thoughts and observations.

He captures all the drama of the sneak attack: the splash of the men wading across the river, the hammer blows of men building a pontoon bridge. The enemy waits high up on the ridges. Then there are the command officers huddled in

Capa covers the Republic's desperate struggles in the Ebro.

caves, strategizing. In the morning, the commander gives the men a short speech like a political rally. "Words are hardly necessary," Capa explains, "since everyone knows what is at stake."

Then we see the line of men, rifles in hand, take a bare, rocky hillside, the stretcher bearers following behind. They press upward, even though "the enemy increases its artillery fire from the summit. Twenty grenades rain down on the attackers every minute. In caves and crevices sit the *marineros*," Capa writes. "When a grenade comes very close, they press themselves hard against the rock, bend over, and pull their heads in, and wait for what will happen." The battle explodes in a smoky swirl of gun smoke and billowing dust. Two soldiers aid a

wounded soldier. Capa is there for all of it—even the intimate moment as one soldier leans into another, recording a man's last words: "I want to die. Write my mother and tell her."

Capa's coverage is spectacular war journalism, but when he returns to Paris, he suffers a collapse. "I was so sick that for a while I had an absolute breakdown," he writes his mother. Eventually Capa will rouse himself once more and go to Barcelona.

"THE REFUGEES' LONG ROAD"

Barcelona, the city of joyous revolution that Capa and Taro had photographed just two and a half years before, is in chaos by January 1939. With Franco's forces advancing and encircling the southern half of Spain, people first flee Madrid,

"It is not easy to be in such a place and not be able to do anything except record the suffering that others must endure," wrote Capa as he photographed refugees desperately seeking safety. Here, in mid-January 1939, they are trying to reach Barcelona.

then move on to Valencia, then again on the road to Barcelona. One million refugees will arrive on its streets. Up to this time, the city has been spared the kind of aerial warfare that devastated Madrid. Now it is enduring the same relentless bombing. People are starving, surviving for weeks at a time on gray bags of rice the size of a cigarette pack and a finger-sized piece of salt cod.

In a chilling reprise of Málaga, on a sunny day, Capa watches farmers pushing their laden mule carts from Tarragona, south of the city. Women carry their market bags, baskets balanced on their heads. Seventy thousand are trying to escape to Barcelona. Suddenly a squadron of planes swoops down. "Each bomber had four to eight machine guns spraying bullets like a garden sprinkler in all directions," writes correspondent Herbert Matthews. Capsized carts, strewn belongings, bloodied pavement—still the refugees shamble forward, eyes blank.

Capa's own history of being uprooted, stateless, homeless, is magnified a thousandfold. As he writes in his own caption: this "is the gamble shared by all of the refugees. . . . Everyone on the road is in the hands of Fate with life-and-death stakes."

Capa sees the same exodus spreading throughout Europe and Asia: "Hundreds and hundreds of thousands I have seen flee thus, in two nations, Spain and China. And I am afraid that hundreds of thousands more, who in other countries perhaps are still living comfortable lives, may soon find themselves enduring the same fate. That is what in recent years has happened to this world in which we wanted to live."

Late January: Capa records the refugees as they stream out of Barcelona toward France.

On the road to France.

As winter descends, four hundred thousand will struggle to the border of France. They know to remain in Spain means risking the vengeance of Franco's troops and possible death. A column of exhausted loyalist soldiers, dirty blankets hung over their shoulders to battle the icy winds, make their way to the wire fences, behind which hastily assembled barracks will form the basis of refugee camps. Exhausted, depressed, Capa cannot bear to photograph any more of Spain.

By April 1, 1939, the war in Spain is over. Franco has won.

FLORIDA, MARCH 1939

Back in Key West, Hemingway separates from his wife and now lives with Martha Gellhorn. She writes and publishes some of the finest war journalism about Spain. Like Taro and Capa and Chim, she focuses on ordinary people, the wry and tragic ways they adapt to war. She tells of flower sellers in Barcelona

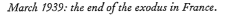

March 1939: the end of the exodus in France.

Though it dates from 1937, this Regards *cover predicts the outcome of the war: triumphant fascism in Spain sealing out Loyalist refugees.*

who, after one bombing, provide for so many funerals that they have nothing left for the victims of the next attack.

Gellhorn and Hemingway take up residence in a crumbling villa in Cuba, where after seventeen feverish months, Hemingway finishes *For Whom the Bell Tolls*. Into this manuscript he pours everything he has seen—the hope and heroism, the betrayals, the cynical manipulation by the Soviets. He is not just a partisan anymore. He is a novelist passionately devoted to telling the truth. The novel will be published in 1940 to tremendous critical and commercial success. However, the Left—the International Brigades especially—feel abandoned by Hemingway, their former hero, the celebrity fighting for their cause. They wanted a tale of the heroic fight against fascist evil, not a dark story that fearlessly explores everyone's brutality. The Abraham Lincoln Brigade boycotts the book and tells everyone not to read it.

PARIS, AUGUST—OCTOBER 1939

On August 23, the Soviet Union and Nazi Germany sign a nonaggression pact—in effect they are now allies. This is the worst betrayal for those on the Left who went to Spain to fight fascism. A nervous French government shuts down communist publications such as *Ce Soir*, fearing they might follow Stalin's lead and take on a new, pro-Nazi stance.

It is no longer safe for Capa to remain in Europe. In May, Chim was given an assignment to photograph a boat filled with Spanish refugees headed to Mexico, which is granting asylum to many from the Spanish Republic, including its leaders. Chim's assignment was a ticket to safety. Capa had no visa and could not join his friend.

At the studio on rue Froidevaux, Cziki Weisz, Capa's old friend from Hungary and darkroom assistant, has been carefully organizing boxes to house the thousands and thousands of images Capa, Taro, and Chim have made in these years during the Spanish Civil War. Each compartment in the boxes holds a spool of tightly wound film; on the inside of the lids is a grid with the films labeled according to what battle or subject was shot. Another box has envelopes with sheaves of cut-up negatives, also labeled.

Before Chim left, he helped arrange the negatives, and now Capa and Weisz finish as best they can. They know they must work swiftly, for any day now war will break out.

On September 1, 1939, the Nazis invade Poland, using the military tactics that they honed in Spain. After years of saber rattling, the annexation of Czechoslovakia, and belligerent war speeches, the worst has happened. The dark shadow that the artists had all warned about back in the Paris cafés has come true: war has come to Europe. Two days later England and France declare war on Germany.

The French government starts to round up German émigrés and leading communists for internment. Now it is extremely dangerous for Capa to remain in France. Not only is he Jewish, but he is a photographer whose work was featured in leftist publications. Since Capa is stateless, without a country, passport, or papers, he can only get a visa to enter a new land if he finds a nation to sponsor him. The French turn him down because of his affiliation with *Ce Soir.* Finally he is able to get a visa to the United States through the Chilean consul, the poet Pablo Neruda, now in Paris. The staff of *Time-Life* also intervenes on his behalf. Capa leaves the boxes of negatives in the care of Weisz, and on October 15, as the German forces draw nearer to Paris, he sets sail for New York City.

BLITZKREIG—lightning strike—comes to Europe. The familiar scenes of German Condor squadrons swarming the skies and bombing mercilessly in Spain are now repeated in Belgium and the Netherlands. Europe is convulsing with all those who must flee from their homes. Hundreds of thousands of refugees scatter to the streets and clog the roads toward France. But the Nazis are advancing on Paris—exactly what Capa and Taro and all their friends meeting, talking, writing, marching, taking photos in the years prior had hoped to stop.

This is how Cziki Weisz remembers those dark, dangerous days: Knowing he would be targeted by the Nazis, Weisz puts the boxes of negatives into a rucksack and travels to Bordeaux, in the southwest of France, to try to put them on a ship to Mexico. There he meets a Chilean in the street and asks him to take the film packages to his consulate for safekeeping. The man agrees.

Weisz bicycles away.

The images, the negatives, are lost.

On June 4, 1944, Capa is ready for the action to come. The images in this chapter through page 225 were all taken by Capa in the following days and months.

CHAPTER SEVENTEEN

"THE MOST IMPORTANT STORY OF THE CENTURY"

JUNE 6, 1944

CAPA REMEMBERS waking under a coarse blanket, inside a swaying ship hold. His camera bag is beside him. A young man, a survivor of the first wave of amphibious crafts that made it to the Normandy beaches, lies beside him, also recovering.

Then it all comes back to Capa: the day gray like dirty laundry; the young men who had bravely clambered off boats and waded into the foaming water as German troops pounded them with mortar and machine-gun fire from the cliffs above. This is D-Day—when thousands of troops, vehicles, and tanks are crossing the English Channel to the beaches of Normandy, the "greatest amphibious assault ever attempted." Capa can still hear the shells exploding in the water; see the fallen and dead bodies strewn in the tide;

A Catholic priest celebrates Mass shortly after D-Day, when the beach is secured.

recall how he had crouched behind one of the X-shaped barriers, snapping away until he was shaking with fear. Then he waded the fifty feet back to a small craft, waves slapping his face, cameras held high over his head. Back on the deck of the USS *Samuel Chase*, he photographed the dead and wounded. And then, nothing. He had collapsed from exhaustion.

When Capa's boat lands back in England a few hours later, he is surrounded by a mob of reporters, all of whom want to hear about the momentous invasion. Capa, however, gives the film to an army officer who will give it to a courier, turns right around, and boards the next boat back to Normandy.

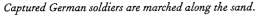
Captured German soldiers are marched along the sand.

JUNE 7, 1944

Life picture editor John Morris remembers June 7 as one of the longest days of his life, pacing his London office, waiting impatiently for Capa's pictures of the D-Day

As the Allies push into Normandy, a German officer surrenders.

invasion to arrive by courier. He knows this is "the most important story of the century." If the magazine has any photos at all, Capa will have taken them. That is, if Capa himself survived.

Morris has set up a complicated procedure for printing Capa's pictures, getting the images past the censor, then on the first flight out to the U.S., to make the June 12 issue, which is already printing in New York. "I felt . . . that the whole world was waiting on these pictures," Morris will recall.

Photos from other photographers have come in, but they are background images; none are close-up action shots of the invasion. The hours drag on. The entire staff is tense and coiled, waiting to spring into action. Finally, they receive

A soldier sings, surrounded by French townspeople. Capa looked both for the heat of combat and for moments of human connection.

An exhausted American GI rests ten days after D-Day.

a call from the coast of England: the film is on its way. Soon the pouch arrives by motorcycle courier.

"Rush, rush, rush!" Morris barks to the darkroom assistant.

A few minutes later, the assistant comes back in tears. "They're ruined! Ruined!"

Something went wrong. Whether it was the splash of waves, camera jams, or perhaps the darkroom heat, out of the three or four rolls Capa took, only ten shots are salvageable. But they are still extraordinary. Even the melting creates an intense effect: blurred shots of men wading through the churning waters of Normandy beaches, lying belly down in the surf, ducking behind spindly, X-shaped barriers.

Over three and a half million readers will open their magazines to see the headline: BEACHHEADS OF NORMANDY: THE FATEFUL BATTLE FOR EUROPE IS JOINED BY SEA AND AIR. The photographs are instantly legendary.

Capa will go on to photograph the cleared Omaha Beach three days later, the slow and dangerous operations as Allied troops make their way through the booby-trapped villages of Normandy, General Charles de Gaulle's triumphant march at the liberation of Paris, the Battle of the Bulge, and the liberation of Leipzig—Taro's home. There Capa takes another photo of a soldier, shot nearly at the moment of death, just as he did a few years before on the autumn slopes in Spain. Now he captures a young American just after he is picked off by a sniper and slumps to the floor of a balcony.

When Paris was liberated in August 1944, Capa came across a tank with Teruel *scrawled on the side, manned by Spanish refugees from the Civil War who had joined the resistance and were leading the way into Paris. Capa told them in Spanish that he had photographed the Battle of Teruel (see page 106), and they let him go on ahead.*

MAGNUM

In the spring of 1947, two years after the end of World War II, Capa and several others gather in the penthouse of the Museum of Modern Art in New York City. They are here to hammer out the details of a new idea: a photographers' collective. Joining Capa is Maria Eisner, who headed the agency for which Taro and Capa once worked. Henri Cartier-Bresson and Chim are traveling, but they have agreed to be part of the team.

The idea is to create an agency for and by photographers. They will pool their resources, generate stories, and control more of the terms in their dealings with magazines. These ideals harken back to the 1930s when they were all leaning on one another—sharing tips, money, cameras—and trying to work out new ideas about politics and art.

Now seasoned in his dealings with publications, Capa wants the photographer to be in charge, not just chasing after the ideas dreamed up by magazine editors. The group divides up coverage of the world: Chim takes Europe; Cartier-Bresson is headed to India and the Far East; an English photographer, George Rodger, will cover Africa and the Middle East; and Bill Vandivert will photograph the United States. Capa will roam at large. They will have offices in New York City and in Paris. Most groundbreaking—they will hold on to the ownership, or copyright, of their pictures. No longer will magazine editors be able to chop up photographs as they wish; no longer will photographers lose their work once it is printed. A photo is as personal as a painting or a poem.

"Why be exploited by others?" Capa tells his good friend Gisèle Freund. "Let's exploit ourselves."

On that day in 1947, upstairs in the fancy penthouse, they christen their agency "Magnum." Later, no one can quite recall how they came up with the name—one suggestion is they opened up a magnum bottle of champagne.

Capa's image of a destroyed church in Normandy stands for all the devastation left behind by the fighting.

Robert Capa in Israel, the handsome, relaxed man of the world.

For Capa, who has always lived for freedom yet who understands the necessity of friendship and comradeship, Magnum is a surprisingly elegant solution: a collective that protects the photographer. And the gregarious, restless Capa now has a perfect role; he is always calling up editors or photographers, making arrangements, suggesting stories. His "meetings" are often held at a Parisian bar where he would play pinball, a cigarette dangling from his mouth as he talks— that is, before he is off on an assignment of his own.

He is a world-famous photographer; he stands for the very term *war photographer.* Capa has become "Bob," the handsome, dark-eyed hero who has been everywhere. He goes to Hollywood and dates movie star Ingrid Bergman, crafts a photo essay on the Soviet Union with the American author John Steinbeck, photographs the birth of the nation of Israel. Capa is a perpetual rover, rubbing elbows with authors and celebrities, or happily playing poker on an oil drum in some remote locale.

Capa visited Israel three times. In the spring of 1949, he recorded the joyous arrival of refugees. The creation of the state of Israel gave him a sense of hope after the traumas he had lived through and witnessed since the 1930s.

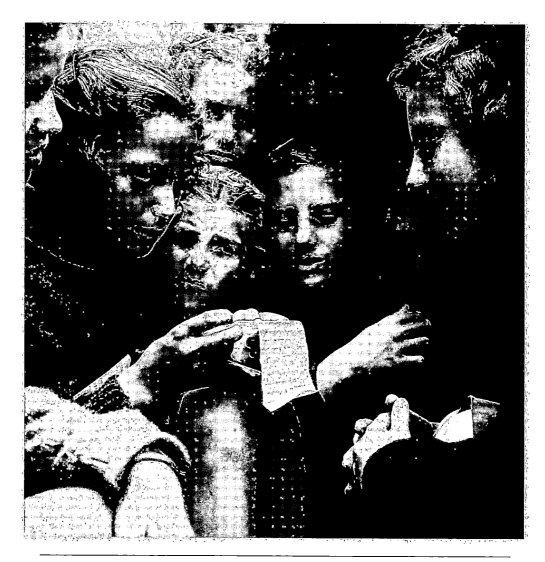

Having lost his parents and much of his family in the Holocaust, the bespectacled, quiet Chim became a wanderer, a photographer of children, war, refugees, and movie stars. In 1948, Chim went on assignment for UNESCO to document child survivors of World War II. This was taken in Greece.

BY 1953, CAPA IS TIRED. Despite his fame and the fees he can command for his work, he is broke. Money still leaks from his pockets. He is drinking too much, uninspired by his glamorous and fluffy assignments. He itches to get back into action. Yet he's also making noises about giving up photography altogether. "It's not a job for a grown man to click a camera," he remarks. But what can he do? This is all he knows. On his fortieth birthday in October, he says morosely, "I can't be forty, how can anybody be forty? I don't know how I'm going to do it."

He is tired of war, too. He even confides, "If I have to go to war again, I'll shoot myself because I've seen too much." The cost of war is finally catching up with the older Capa.

Then, in early 1954, he gets a call that cheers him: a long assignment in Japan. While there, he is tempted by yet another possibility—covering the situation in Indochina, where communist guerrillas, the Vietminh, are gaining ground

In 1954, Capa found a welcome in Japan, where he recorded another kind of new beginning.

*In May 1954, Capa walks with
a French military doctor in Laos.
Photograph by Michel Descamps.*

against colonial French forces. The French, like the English, have long ruled world-spanning empires. But the Europeans are losing their grip. Here in Asia, it seems the colonial masters may finally be overthrown. The assignment is dangerous, but the money is tempting, as is the chance to get in on the next big war.

On May 25, 1954, carrying a flask of cognac and a thermos of iced tea, Capa sets out with an army convoy making its way through the Red River delta. Wearing a khaki jacket, trousers, and a jaunty cap, with two cameras slung around his neck, Capa looks out at the emerald-green rice fields. Occasionally he clambers off a jeep to photograph peasants stooped over their crop. Now and then gunfire opens up, flashing in the waving grass. The muggy heat wraps like a blanket. Explosions thud nearby. A convoy up the road is ambushed. The Vietminh are everywhere, it seems.

Capa is energized, back into combat mode. Bored with staying in a slow-moving jeep, he decides to risk it and see what's ahead. "I'm going up the road a little bit," he tells a lieutenant. "Look for me when you get started again." Capa walks along the road, down into a swampy stream and back toward the advancing soldiers. He snaps shots from both his cameras—one in color, one in black and white.

Just as he's climbing back up toward the road, he steps on a land mine and is flung to the ground. His leg is blown off, his chest gouged.

Robert Capa is the first journalist killed in the war in Indochina.

This is among the last shots Capa took. "I realize now that he died for the world. . . . I lost him and hope the world will gain some truth and humanity from this life," wrote Julia Friedmann about her son Robert Capa.

CHAPTER EIGHTEEN

WHAT REMAINS?

ONE COULD SAY they failed.

By 1956, twenty years after Capa and Taro met their friends at a café, then headed to join the thousands at the Place de la République, two decades after they dared to get on a plane to photograph Spain's living revolution, they are dead, as is their friend Chim, tragically killed, perhaps by friendly fire in Sinai that year.

Capa and Taro and Chim lost their lives, and lost in Spain. The photographers did not sway hearts and minds—or at least not enough to get governments to intervene on behalf of the Republic. Franco came to rule for nearly forty years. Spain itself is still divided and conflicted about this history. The very church square in Brunete that Taro photographed now proudly displays a monument to the brutal Falangists who fought on Franco's side. The full revelation of Stalin's crimes soured many people on the heroic story of the Spanish Civil War. With all the betrayals, the assassinations, the imprisonments, what endures?

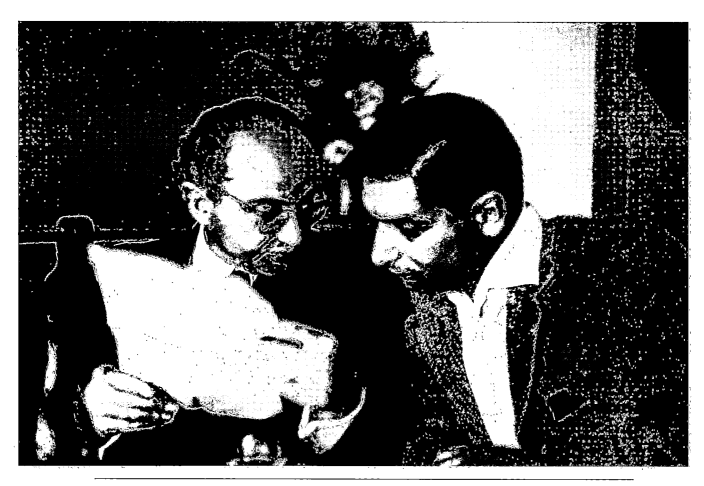

Chim and Capa—a study in contrasts as personality types—bonded in their work as photographers and friends. This photo was taken in 1952 by Henri Cartier-Bresson, a third member of the original Magnum team.

Magnum has survived to become a part of Capa's ongoing story. It runs as a collective, whose members are voted in, and it includes many of the best photojournalists of our time. Even if the agency sometimes functions like a cranky family, with squabbles and rickety financing, to this day Magnum stands for the finest photojournalism in the world. The tradition continues.

Something else endures. It is not just that Magnum still provides a home for photojournalists—there are many kinds of photo agencies now, and new ways for photographers to own and share their materials. An idea was born in those key years in the 1930s, when Capa and Taro were young and penniless, seeking to make their mark, when young people everywhere were trying to sort out the conflicts of the individual and the group: the value of friendship and cooperation.

Collaboration, teamwork—all this harks back to Capa's relationship with Taro and his connections with Chim and Cartier-Bresson. They understood that even as they were solitary seekers of images, they were part of a whole. Capa and Taro found a balance together as lovers, *copains*, colleagues carrying equipment, dividing up the scenes they shot. And behind them, in Paris, was Cziki Weisz, the quiet photographer in the darkroom, printing the images that they reaped from the wilds of war. They all were needed; they all had a role to play.

Inside the legend that became Robert Capa is the scruffy young man who walked up to a strange girl in a Paris café and found the love of his life in her friend; the young man who went to Spain with Taro, the woman who not only shared his life but helped to create it. Though Taro vanished from sight, she was never really gone. As her biographer Irme Schaber explains, it was as if Taro became part of Capa. Her memory, her heritage, the intense days they spent collaborating, shaped him. They were explorers, creators, together. Spain was his baptism into this terrifying profession—a profession they helped to invent and for which they both gave their lives.

Fifty-six years after their images were last seen in a bicycle pouch, it turns out pictures live on, too.

The dapper Capa looking like a movie star, with a teasing glint in his eye. This photo was taken in 1952 by another accomplished photographer, Ruth Orkin.

CHAPTER NINETEEN

TO SEE

MEXICO CITY, 1995

AT AN EXHIBIT of photographs of the Spanish Civil War, a man tentatively approaches Jerald R. Green, a professor of Spanish and Mexican art. He tells Professor Green that he believes he has more than two thousand negatives by Robert Capa, who has been dead for over forty years.

For decades Cornell Capa, Robert's younger brother, desperately searched for the lost cache of negatives. Cornell tried everything, from advertising in a French magazine to pursuing leads while on a trip to South America. Legend has it that a group even dug up a garden where the negatives were rumored to be buried. Cornell adopted his brother's last name in tribute and also became a photographer with *Life* magazine. In 1974, he founded the International Center for Photography (ICP).

Now there is the mysterious Benjamin Tarver in Mexico City, claiming he might have Cornell's brother's negatives—the ones that disappeared after Cziki Weisz handed them off. Slowly, fitfully, through letters, a conversation begins. Finally in 2007, Trisha Ziff, a documentary filmmaker living in

Mexico City who is acting on Cornell's behalf, meets Tarver at a coffee shop. There, Tarver shows her three contact sheets that clearly come from Capa's negatives. She is stunned.

The pieces of the story are put together: at some point the boxes of negatives were turned over to General Francisco Aguilar González, the Mexican ambassador to the French government in 1941 or 1942. During the Spanish Civil War,

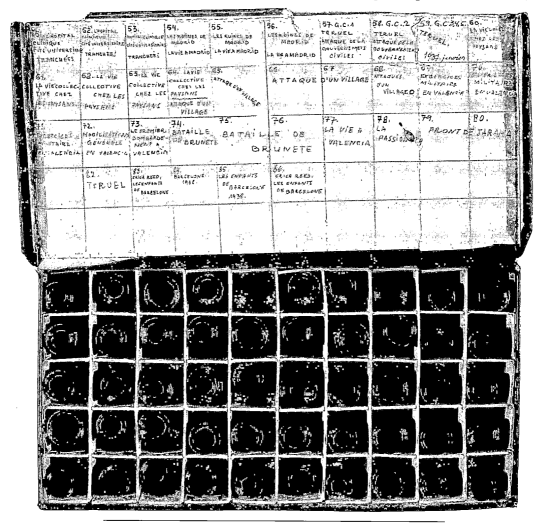

From the Mexican Suitcase, this box holds labeled rolls of negatives.

Mexico had supported the Spanish Republic, sending over ammunition and other supplies. As the war ended, and Spaniards were stranded in camps on the coast of France, the Mexicans reached out and offered asylum. As Chim recorded in May 1939, over twenty thousand sailed to Mexico and made it their home rather than stay in Spain, where they might be shot or imprisoned. More than one hundred thousand refugees would eventually come to settle in Mexico.

The general's daughter, Graciela Aguilar de Ona, knew Tarver as a close family friend; one day she pulled him aside, opened a plastic bag, and showed the boxes to Tarver, asking him what she should do. This prompted him to approach the professor at the exhibition of Spanish Civil War photographs.

Ironically, Cziki Weisz eventually settled in Mexico City. He lived just a mile away from the general, where the lost boxes lay hidden in an old armoire.

In December 2007, the negatives arrive in New York City in their cardboard boxes. Miraculously, because of the temperate weather in Mexico, the negatives are in near-perfect condition. Slowly, with white gloves, the curators at ICP slip the negatives out of their compartments and unwind the tightly wound spools. Some of the negatives from Mexico exactly line up with those that were missing from Capa's, Taro's, and Chim's notebooks. "Two disparate pieces of a jigsaw puzzle," explains Brian Wallis, the head curator.

The curators cannot believe their good luck. And, just a few months before he passes away, Cornell is able to touch the original film of his brother's early work in Europe and Spain.

There are 4,500 images in all.

WITNESS

And so the photographs live on. The lost images, in a way, became refugees just like Capa, like so many photographers—winding their way across oceans and continents, in flight from their origins, bearing witness to all they have seen and experienced. They are the residue that washes up after this terrible history has subsided—the testimony that allows us to see.

Even for those who came to doubt the Left, the Spanish Civil War remained a pure struggle, a pure time in their lives. As Orwell would write: "Curiously enough the whole experience has left me with not less but more belief in the decency of human beings."

Despite the failure of their cause, all of them—the journalists such as Gellhorn, Orwell, Capa himself—looked at the Spanish Civil War as the most idealistic time of their lives. In Spain they discovered themselves as vital, dynamic young people, tasted freedom, stepped out of the routine of their lives to glimpse a vision of a more egalitarian society.

Pepita Carpena, who joined the anarchist party in Barcelona as a teenager in the early days of the fight, reflects: "We lived those years intensely. It was constant struggle, revolution, emancipation . . . where you realize that freedom is necessary."

"Youth was born in Spain," Jay Allen wrote. He meant that, being young, one could envision—and fight for—a better world.

Now restored, these photographs remind us of what was so crucial and important about that moment in history. The Spanish Civil War, as everyone feared, was a prelude to World War II. By the end of that war, the devastation was beyond understanding: the Holocaust, the atomic bomb, the millions upon millions of deaths. All over Europe children were crawling around the rubble of a civilization. In Poland alone, 1.7 million children were orphaned as a result of World War II. Millions more were homeless.

In 1955, ten years after the war ended, the Museum of Modern Art opened a photography show, *The Family of Man*, which culled images from all over the world, grouped in themes such as romance, weddings, childhood, mother and child, death. It was as if to say that after the world was ripped apart by political

The Family of Man *exhibit celebrated the essential stages of life as experienced by peoples and cultures throughout the world. The exhibit included Chim's 1948 photo showing children in shattered Italy after the war and Cartier-Bresson's 1948 image from India depicting faith.*

divisions, ideologies, race, ethnicity, it was time for finding universal bonds that all humans share. A father in Bechuanaland (now Botswana) in Africa teaching his son to spear-hunt is no different from one in Austria playing a clarinet while his son follows with a recorder. "We shall be one person," reads one of the captions.

Photography, the singular image, created a vocabulary for traumatic, cataclysmic events. Capa—indeed, all of the Magnum photographers—knew this. Like deep-sea divers, they plunged right into the waves that crashed across our globe and came back with their shimmering fish, their pictures. Photographs became our way of understanding the modern world—they take what is abstract, overwhelming, and bring it concretely into the human, the comprehensible.

No doubt, much of what Taro and Capa accomplished during the Spanish

Civil War had the tinge and tone of propaganda. The photographs they took were clearly partisan during a time—the 1930s—when the world was fiercely divided. *Death in the Making*, the 1938 photography book that Capa published, reads like a political tract. Capa's and Taro's and Chim's work was featured prominently in several pamphlets that circulated internationally, showing the plight of the Spanish Republic.

And yet they—like many of the young people who went over to Spain—were often confronted with the enemy's humanity. When Aleksander Szurek saw his "first fascist corpse," he was startled, almost surprised at the beauty of the fallen young man. As a communist, he'd had drummed into him "the mere fact that he's a capitalist, he's ugly." In this instant, his ideology was shaken; he identified with another young man, who also came far for a terrible war: "Yet this fascist seemed handsome. Could he have left relatives?"

During the Spanish Civil War, neither Capa nor Taro allowed the rumbles and splits that were taking place in the Left to deter them from going out and photographing. As his brother, Cornell, recalled, Capa "was just as much against oppression of the Left as he was against oppression of the Right."

Between two domineering ideologies—communism and fascism—was a gap, a space of breathing, of hope, into which young people rushed. Too many were crushed, killed, exiled. And yet there was also a truth that they glimpsed; something new was being born: we emerged into a postwar period in which we tried to repair our sundered world. We tried to see the handsome enemy. After Spain, Capa did not flinch from showing the ugliness of "his side." After World War II, one of his most painful, humane shots is of a French woman with a shaved head carrying her baby, jeered and denounced by crowds for having had a relationship with a German soldier.

The photography these young people invented opened up the world for us to see, to feel. That ripple has since spread onward—in the historic *Family of Man* exhibit; in *Life* magazine, which would go on to chronicle the great upheavals of the twentieth century; in the entire profession of photo- and war journalism. Every year the Overseas Press Club of America presents the Robert Capa Gold Medal Award to the "best published photographic reporting from abroad requiring exceptional courage and enterprise."

All of this can be traced back to that moment in Spain when this band of young people set off with their new lightweight cameras. Now ordinary people could see images of ordinary civilians thousands of miles away being pummeled by war. The far off, the invisible, the distant, became as real as one's own life.

Capa's image of the French woman with a shaved head. The 1944 photo centers on the vulnerable woman and her baby; it is not arguing for one side of the conflict or the other.

This is the true impact of photography, one that endures today, where news photos spill into our smartphones and social media feeds.

Capa and Taro gave us a visual language for understanding the catastrophic changes, the disasters and tragedies, of the first half of the twentieth century. No one had seen anything like this, nor brought back such a record of witnessing. They, like writers, made sense of this massive devastation by homing in on the particular: a refugee girl, with her neat bangs, resting on her suitcase in Barcelona; a soldier reading a newspaper on a deck chair, next to a barricade of sandbags.

These images have a way of piercing through the fog of rhetoric and cheery exhortations. These are faces, human faces—lined, sorrowful, tired, stoic, shamed. Decent. These are real children, real mothers, and real fathers. This is the power of photography. This is what photographers are willing to do: risk their own lives, go into the fire, and emerge like sorcerers with the magic eye of seeing. To see, to tell, to bear witness. In a single image.

They gave birth to the visual world we live in now. They urge us to do the same.

Go. Go witness. Go see. And show us all you have seen.

APPENDIX A

THE CONTROVERSY OVER *THE FALLING SOLDIER*

From the moment Capa's shot of the dying soldier appeared in print, it served as the poster image of the Spanish Civil War. But in 1975 Phillip Knightley, a British author who was interested in carefully investigating war reporting, made a startling claim. He had interviewed O. D. Gallagher, a journalist who knew Capa in Spain. Gallagher insisted that the day after Capa took the photo, as they shared too many drinks, Capa admitted that he had staged the shot—it was a fake, not a real image of a man at the moment of death.

Gallagher's indictment shook Capa's fans and split experts on photography and the war. Some quickly dismissed the journalist as a drunken hack misremembering, or even inventing, a conversation from long ago. After all, Gallagher was nowhere near Capa the day the photograph was taken and was, in fact, covering the fascist side. Over time others, who were growing more skeptical of the entire story of the heroic Left—especially after the fall of the Soviet

Union, when more details about Stalin's role in Spain became public—were happy to see the favorite image of the Left challenged. Capa's fraud, if it was that, seemed to symbolize all the tattered, unraveling myths and legends of the "good" fight against fascism.

Richard Whelan devoted a good part of his professional life to researching Capa's biography. Though he was drawn to the task because he admired Capa, Whelan was a serious, fair-minded, and extremely thorough and conscientious scholar. In 2007, the year he died, he published a chapter in a book devoted to Capa's Spanish Civil War photos in which he carefully weighed the evidence. While it was easy to question Gallagher, it was also true that Capa had given a variety of accounts of where, when, and how the photo was taken. These stories did not all line up. Whelan could not say for certain how the shot was taken. Still, based on his research, the argument was made that it was taken in Cerro Muriano and that by matching that location with the records of troop movements, one could actually identify the very man who had been killed that day. So the debate stood on Whelan's death.

Since then, however, a Spanish scholar has raised important new questions. Examining the slope of the hills, the movement of clouds, he saw that the image was not taken in Cerro Muriano, so the soldier killed there could not be the man in the photo. We can now say the photo was taken near the village of Espejo, and there are no records of firefights in that location on that day.

This, then, is the case against the photo: we know for certain that Capa, Taro, and Chim staged scenes to shoot. That was accepted practice. And unless new evidence emerges, we cannot name a clash of arms or identify a government soldier killed on that day. The possibility of a staged shot cannot be rejected.

The case for the image, though, is strong. Capa never claimed he was covering a battle, and there were shots, snipers, and friendly fire everywhere in Spain during the war. The account of the shot that seemed to carry the most emotional weight for Capa was one in which he was responsible for the man's death. Rather than staging an event, on that afternoon Capa, Taro, and the soldiers were being playful. Perhaps at one moment Capa asked a soldier to stand up, or to come over a hilltop, and just then a sniper picked him off. This fits what two experts accustomed to analyzing forensic evidence told Whelan. They concluded that the way the man is falling could not be faked and is, instead, exactly how a man shot through the heart would react. In this view, Capa did not stage a fake death, but he felt he had put the soldier in harm's way.

This is what current evidence can tell us, but there is a larger question of truth. Whatever happened before, or during, the taking of that exact shot, Capa made a point of being close enough to the action to capture everything, even the moment of death. If it wasn't this man at that moment, it might well have been another. He and Taro risked everything, gave everything, to be as close as possible to the action. Never before could the world get such an immediate, vivid image of the price of war. That is the enduring truth of this solider as he falls.

APPENDIX B

THE CONTROVERSY OVER THE DEATH OF OLIVER LAW

For those who see the fight to defeat Franco, particularly the service of the International Brigades, as an expression of idealism and heroism, the story of Oliver Law is especially powerful. That a committed African American led integrated troops in Spain—which had never taken place before in U.S. history—shows what the fight was all about. Law and his fellow soldiers gave their lives to combating racism and injustice. Yet just as with *The Falling Soldier*, there is a counterstory about Law's death and a controversy over which tale to believe. As with everything about the Spanish Civil War, debates about matters of fact quickly become judgments of belief, trust, and politics.

Toward the end of his life, Paul Robeson tried to make a film about Law—in his eyes the perfect hero. The June 2009 issue of *The Volunteer*, a magazine founded by veterans of the Abraham Lincoln Brigade, tells the story of Robeson in Spain, including Oliver Law's life and death, in a graphic novel [alba.valb.org].

But two veterans of the brigade who served with Law at Brunete later claimed that the heroic story was wrong. Law, they insisted, was killed by his own men, either because they did not accept being led by an African American or because he was so incompetent or reckless that only by eliminating him could they save their own lives. The sequence of claims and counterclaims was explored by the Abraham Lincoln Brigade Archives (ALBA). The veterans' organization concluded that the two vets had become fervent anticommunists after learning of Stalin's crimes. Perhaps for that reason they wanted to undermine the story of Law's heroism and the triumph over racism that his leadership represented.

While ALBA's article lists all the twists and turns of the debate, it is not entirely convincing. The fact that the killed-by-his-own-men accusation changed over time, and came in different forms, does not mean it was entirely invented. Both the veterans who told the heroic story and those who denied it were known to be truthful men. But there is also another factor to consider. Throughout the war the Soviets used the brigades as cannon fodder—driving them to exhaustion and putting them in positions to take extremely heavy losses. If Law, as the leading officer, risked too much in trying to take a hill from the enemy, he was being exactly the kind of leader the Soviets demanded. Rather than arguing over who killed Law, we might look at both stories as true: the idealism of the brigade gave him a chance to lead; the callous brutality of the Soviets made it likely he would die.

APPENDIX C

THE SYRIAN CIVIL WAR AND THE SPANISH CIVIL WAR

As of this writing, the leader of Syria is Bashar al-Assad, whose father, Hafiz al-Assad, was in power from 1971 to 2000. The elder Assad was famously intelligent, crafty, and murderous. While his son was educated in the West, and many hoped he would begin a reform of his country, by 2011 a rebellion had broken out against his rigid regime. The government fought back and has been accused by the United Nations of using poison gas against its own people.

Should the world intervene in Syria? The situation in the country is dire. Hundreds of thousands of civilians have been killed, and millions of Syrians have fled the country. This flood of vulnerable, desperate people has become a humanitarian crisis of its own. The only way to allow the people of Syria to live safely in their homeland is to end the war. The problem is that Assad is backed by Russia and Iran, who will block any effort in the United Nations to take strong action. And the fight against Assad is no longer reform-minded rebels against an oppressive government. In many parts of Syria, the most active and successful fighters are allied with the group that calls itself the Islamic State—a barbaric anti-Western terrorist organization. Indeed, as the civil war renders parts of Syria and neighboring Iraq ungovernable, the Islamic State has made itself into a kind of government.

If the West tries to support the fight against bloody Assad, it risks aiding the even more gruesome Islamic State. If the United States or Europe sides with Assad, it will be supporting a leader we have said must be removed for crimes against his own people. That is the state of the conflict as of this morning's news. However the conflict eventually plays out, the situation in Syria has led many to look back to the Spanish Civil War.

In 1936, to allow Franco to win was to let Hitler grow stronger. To oppose Franco was to side with the equally murderous Stalin. And yet—now as in the late 1930s—when the world does nothing, the situation gets worse. The Islamic State has expanded and trained or inspired terrorists in many lands, including France and the United States. The fight in Syria is becoming a regional and even international struggle.

The choice between unappealing allies is not the only link between Syria and Spain. In Spain, when the Western powers refused to take a stand against fascism, volunteers came on their own. In Syria, as the great powers of the world are stalemated, the Islamic State actively recruits men and women to join its ranks. Of course, Syria is the reverse of Spain: instead of individuals risking everything to fight tyranny, an explicitly brutal regime brainwashes young people to kill and die for them. But there is a parallel: when the world community cannot act, global issues become personal choices. We seem to be reliving a nightmare version of another generation's experiences.

There are two ways the story of Spain may help us think about Syria: nations chose not to be involved in Spain—preferring nonintervention to supporting one horrific murderer over another—and paid the price when a larger war followed. The longer Syria festers, the wider the area of conflict grows. History may not repeat itself—but perhaps it does issue warnings. At the very least, the similarities between Syria and Spain remind us that the past is not dead. Rather, it is there to give us a portrait, a model, of causes and consequences, choices and outcomes.

On a second, more hopeful and humanistic note, individuals who went to Spain made use of their talents to explore their experiences. Capa and Taro, Chim, Picasso, Neruda and Hughes, Hemingway and Orwell, and many others transformed tragedy into enduring art. Perhaps the pain of the Syrian war will bring new voices that all of us need to hear.

CAST OF CHARACTERS

INDIVIDUALS

PHOTOGRAPHERS

ROBERT CAPA (1913–1954), born André Friedmann, in Budapest, Hungary

HENRI CARTIER-BRESSON (1908–2004), born in Chanteloup-en-Brie, France; much-honored French photographer known for his idea that the photographer can capture the "decisive moment"

DAVID SEYMOUR CHIM (1911–1956), born David Syzmin, in Warsaw, Poland

ANDRÉ KERTÉSZ (1894–1985), born in Budapest, Hungary; Robert Capa's mentor, who eventually settled in New York City

FRED STEIN (1909–1967), born in Dresden, Germany; member of Capa and Taro's circle in Paris; managed to reach New York, where he had a long career as a photographer

GERDA TARO (1910–1937), born Gerta Pohorylle, in Stuttgart, Germany

WRITERS, JOURNALISTS, NOVELISTS, POETS, MEMOIRISTS, AND ARTISTS

RAFAEL ALBERTI (1902–1999), Spanish poet who sided with the Republic, wrote heroic poems honoring the defense of Madrid, ran Casa de Alianza de Escritores Antifascistas with his wife, María Teresa León, and left the country while Franco was in power

TED ALLAN (1916–1995), Canadian writer who volunteered for the Republic in Spain; his memoir *This Time a Better Earth* is the key account of Taro during the battle of Brunete

JAY ALLEN (1900–1972), American journalist who covered Spain for the *Chicago Tribune*; favored Republic but interviewed Franco and other rebel leaders; translated Capa's captions in his book on Spain, *Death in the Making*

W. H. AUDEN (1907–1973), English poet who briefly volunteered in Spain during the Civil War; later became an American citizen and rejected his earlier leftist beliefs and poems

ARTURO BAREA (1897–1957), a Spaniard who worked as a censor for the Republic and wrote about his experiences in his memoir, *The Forging of a Rebel*

ALVAH BESSIE (1904–1985), American volunteer fighter for the Republic; his memoir *Men in Battle* tells that story; later he worked as a screenwriter but lost his job during the McCarthy period as one of the "Hollywood 10"

CLAUD COCKBURN (1904–1981), British journalist who covered Spain for the *Daily Worker*, a communist newspaper

VIRGINIA COWLES (1912–1983), American journalist who reported from Spain for several papers; she sought to be fair to both sides

JOHN DOS PASSOS (1896–1970), American writer who came to Spain to support the Republic after writing acclaimed pro-Left novels about America in the early twentieth century; disillusioned in Spain, he became increasingly conservative

MARTHA GELLHORN (1908–1998), American journalist who broke ground for female reporters in Spain and later during World War II; favored the Republic

ANDRÉ GIDE (1869–1951), French novelist and later Nobel Prize winner who became a communist but after visiting the Soviet Union in 1936 changed his mind; this shift upset defenders of Stalin and the Republic

JOSEPHINE HERBST (1892–1969), journalist and novelist, sympathetic to the Republic

ERNEST HEMINGWAY (1899–1961), American novelist who came to Spain to support the Republic; *For Whom the Bell Tolls*, his novel about the war, is an artistic triumph and brutally honest about both sides; he later won the Nobel Prize for literature

LANGSTON HUGHES (1902–1967), American poet who came to Spain as reporter for a Baltimore newspaper; wrote poems about the war

ALFRED KANTOROWICZ (1899–1979), German writer who served in the International Brigades and wrote about it in his *Spanish War Diary*; created a library of Nazi-banned books in Paris to combat the book-burning frenzy of the early 1930s

MARÍA TERESA LEÓN (1903–1988), Spanish writer and activist; helped save artworks in Madrid during the bombing; left Spain with her husband, Rafael Alberti, during Franco's regime

FEDERICO GARCÍA LORCA (1898–1936), leading Spanish poet and playwright executed by Franco's men

HERBERT MATTHEWS (1900–1977), *New York Times* reporter, sympathetic to the Republic

JESSICA MITFORD (1917–1996), British aristocrat who went to Spain and married a cousin who had been in the International Brigades; later in America, she joined and then rejected the Communist Party

PABLO NERUDA (1904–1973), Chilean poet and later Nobel Prize winner who served as a diplomat in Spain for part of the war

GEORGE ORWELL (1903–1950), born Eric Blair, British writer who came to Spain as a fighter for the Republic; his memoir *Homage to Catalonia* is a model of clear writing and honest reporting; he went on to write *Animal Farm* and *1984*

OCTAVIO PAZ (1914–1998), Mexican poet and later Nobel Prize winner who favored the Republic but lost faith in the cause when a friend was murdered by the communists

PABLO PICASSO (1881–1973), Spanish painter often considered the leading 20th century modernist

GUSTAV REGLER (1898–1963), German communist and friend of Hemingway's who served as volunteer in Spain; his book *The Great Crusade* tells that story

STEPHEN SPENDER (1909–1995), British poet who came to Spain as a communist but later, when Stalin made his pact with Hitler, decided he had been wrong

ALEKSANDER SZUREK (1907–1978), Russian communist who served in Spain; his memoir *Shattered Dream* recounts that experience

MILITARY AND POLITICAL LEADERS IN SPAIN

FRANCISCO FRANCO (1892–1975), born in El Ferrol, Spain, leader of rebel forces, later ruler of Spain for thirty-six years

DOLORES IBÁRRURI (1895–1989), La Pasionaria, born near Bilbao, Spain, inspiring and devoted communist who rallied loyalist forces with her speeches; lifetime defender of Stalin

FRANCISCO LARGO CABALLERO (1869–1946), born in Madrid, prime minister of the Spanish Republic from September 1936 to May 1937

JUAN NEGRÍN (1894–1956), born in Canary Islands, prime minister of the Spanish Republic from May 1937 to March 1939

KEY POLITICAL LEADERS OUTSIDE OF SPAIN

LÉON BLUM (1872–1950), first Jewish premier of France; did not have political support to ally France with the Spanish Republic; survived two Nazi concentration camps

ADOLF HITLER (1889–1945), leader of Nazi Germany from 1933 to 1945, responsible for at least seventeen million deaths through concentration camps, enforced marches, and executions

BENITO MUSSOLINI (1883–1945), leader of fascist Italy from 1922 until 1943; not as murderous as Hilter or Stalin, but his invasion of Ethiopia and use of poison gas cost thousands of lives

FRANKLIN DELANO ROOSEVELT (1882–1945), U.S. president from 1933 to 1945; only person to be elected president four times; did not have political support to lead the United States into an active role in European conflicts until after Pearl Harbor

JOSEPH STALIN (1879–1953), leader of the Soviet Union from 1922 until his death; responsible for killing at least fifteen million people through enforced famines and executions

GROUPS

The names of the parties and factions, allies and enemies, involved in the Spanish Civil War can be confusing. Not only was there a seemingly endless set of competing groups within Spain, but the most general terms used for the main opponents reverse the meaning of words as they are typically used today. Here we both define the different sides and explain a bit about their positions.

THE POPULAR FRONT

Communists call their views "scientific socialism." They believe that Karl Marx discovered the secret motor of human history: a series of revolutions that would inevitably lead to the triumph of the working people. The totally unexpected success of the communists who came to power in Russia in 1917 proved, according to them, that their "science" was perfect. They, and only they, knew where, when, and how to bring the people to power. Socialists, who shared their goals but disagreed with their analysis, were considered either fools or agents of the rich and powerful, seeking to hold back the sweep of history. Year after year, the communists saw the socialists as their prime enemies—competitors for the support and allegiance of workers and intellectuals.

This is like the splits within a religion: Catholics, Protestants, and Eastern Orthodox believers are all Christian but have fought terrible wars against each other. In Islam, Shia and Sunni are both Muslim but have long been strident enemies. This deep clash between people with similar ideas was the story of communism and socialism in the twentieth century. But in 1934, as Hitler rose to power in Germany, the Soviet leader Joseph Stalin hit upon a new policy. Communists were to work alongside socialists against their common enemies. In each country, a new coalition called the Popular Front would unite all on the left and bring them to power—then sort out their differences later.

All across Europe—in France, in England, in Spain—and even in America, those on the left had to choose: join the Popular Front or be seen as an ally of the forces of death and darkness. This was not just a choice of allies—it was a moment of hope: the Left, united, marching together, winning elections, challenging big business, could sweep to victory. The new party slogan in the U.S. was "Communism is twentieth-century Americanism." But everyone also knew that the ultimate communist plan was to undermine and eliminate their current, and temporary, allies.

THE TWO MAIN OPPONENTS IN SPAIN

ON THE LEFT: LOYALISTS, REPUBLICANS

The elected government of Spain. As in France, the Popular Front united socialist, communist, anarchist, and moderate liberal groups. Together they barely won the election of 1936 and came into power as the governing coalition of Spain's Second Republic. Ever since the early 1800s, Spain had been in turmoil, with one kind of government soon overturned and replaced by another. Spain shifted among a king or queen ruling alone, a monarch with a strong parliament, a military ruler, or an elected parliament with no king. The first attempt at a government without a king lasted less than a year, between 1873 and 1874. When King Alfonso XIII fled the country in 1931, a second republic was declared. Those who agreed with the ideas and ideals of the Popular Front believed they were fighting to preserve a legally elected government against what today might be called terrorists or insurgents. Thus the term *loyalist* meant defender of the Republic and, at the same time, being sympathetic to the moderate, extreme, or even revolutionary Left. The name *Republican*, which is also used, has nothing in common with the Republican political party in America.

ON THE RIGHT: REBELS, FASCISTS, NATIONALISTS

General Francisco Franco came to head an alliance of groups fighting against the government, against the Left, against anarchists, unions, socialists, and communists. While today a "rebel" might often be seen as some form of radical seeking to bring down a conservative government, in Spain the rebels saw themselves as cleansing the country of radicals in order to establish strong central power in support of tradition and the Catholic Church.

The rebels are sometimes called nationalists. That is because the loyalists were allied with groups of people, such as the Basques and Catalans, who wanted greater political and economic independence, and even to use their own languages instead of Spanish. Franco and his

This powerful facist poster claims that communism makes everyone equal—through a firing squad.

allies aimed to keep Spain together with no regional independence. The question of how much Spain needs to remain united and how much autonomy to allow its regions in language and laws is still highly controversial today. Franco's side was rebelling—as they saw it—to return Spain to its glorious traditions. In that sense you might say they were similar to American Confederate "Rebs," who were fighting, as they claimed, for the America of the farming and slaveholding founding fathers. To use a more recent parallel, both the Taliban in Afghanistan and the Islamic State are rebelling to return women to the home, enforce their view of religious law, and eliminate what they claim are evil outside influences. All of these rebels fight against what they see as an alien, foreign, and modern world to restore a hallowed past. In Spain the call to Catholic tradition explicitly also included condemnation of Jews, communists, and even Freemasons—the secret society interested in progress to which George Washington, Benjamin Franklin, and Wolfgang Amadeus Mozart belonged.

FACTIONS WITHIN EACH SIDE

THE LOYALISTS

In order to win the election of 1936, the Popular Front patched together groups with wildly different views, hopes, and plans for the future. The heart of the alliance was the unions representing landless peasants and factory workers, some of whom were communists, others socialists, and still others anarchists. They joined with moderate business owners, junior army officers, and intellectuals.

One crucial split that reverses expectations involved the communists within the Popular Front. When the election took place, there were many who believed in the ideas of communism, but only a small minority of those voters belonged to the PCE (Partido Comunista de España), the Communist Party of Spain, which was allied with the Soviet Union and took its lead from Moscow. The other communists were either skeptical of the Soviets or actually opposed to them. Some followed the ideas of Leon Trotsky—one of the leaders of

This is the Communist image of unity—workers, farmers, soldiers, and intellectuals joined.

The UGT was a socialist group, CNT, anarchist—this poster sees the former rivals as powerful allies. They were for a time, but were undermined by the communists. Whether the Spanish Republic could have held together if it had defeated Franco is endlessly debated to this day.

the 1917 revolution in Russia, who had split with Joseph Stalin and had fled for his life. (See Robert Capa's photo of Trotsky on page 6). The twist is that the communists allied with Moscow were relative moderates. The Soviets did not want to provoke Germany or alarm England and France by supporting out-and-out revolution in Spain. They wanted Spain to form a moderate Left government and only later become fully communist. The revolutionary communists wanted Spain to become a new kind of nation, a classless utopia, right away. They also did not want the Soviet Union to tell them what to do. In this vision of radical change they were allied with the anarchists, who wanted no central government at all. When the Popular Front won, the PCE was a tiny party. But as the war went on and the Soviets sent men, money, weapons, and spies, the party in Spain grew ever larger and more influential.

THE REBELS

For the duration of the war, Franco managed to quiet the potential rifts within his side. But the rebels were themselves made up of competing and even violently opposed groups. Indeed, some historians think that Franco's coalition might have fallen apart if the war had dragged on. One cluster of groups wanted Spain to return to being a monarchy. Yet even that cause divided Spaniards. Two different royal families had ruled Spain since the 1800s, and each family had its fervent supporters. Franco often spoke about tradition, but for most of his reign he was not in favor of bringing back a king. He admired Benito Mussolini and Adolf Hitler (though he played this down after 1943, when he began to sense that Germany would lose the war) and centered power on himself.

SUPPORT FOR SPAIN FROM OUTSIDE THE COUNTRY

LEFT: INTERNATIONAL BRIGADES

After the 1917 revolution in Russia, the communists established the Comintern to organize and lead communist parties around the world. The Comintern was given its marching orders by the Soviets and, in turn, established the "party line"—the strategies and tactics—for allied parties in other lands. The effort to bring volunteers to fight for the Republic in Spain was organized by the Comintern, but that does not mean individuals who went to Spain were necessarily communists or, even if they were, that they agreed with the policies of the Soviets. However, the Soviet Union did attempt to use volunteer organizations to serve its own ends—for example, by infiltrating spies. Just under fifty thousand people from around the world volunteered and were organized into seven different brigades. The largest group came from

France; the group from the United States numbered approximately 2,800 people. They became known as the Abraham Lincoln Brigade.

Women who could not fight came to Spain to volunteer as nurses or to assist with refugees or orphan relief.

RIGHT

By pure numbers, more men came to fight for Franco than against him, but the vast majority of those soldiers were sent to Spain by their governments; they had no choice. Still, as outlined below, some fighters did volunteer to fight for Franco.

MOROCCO—One more twist in Spain had to do with Morocco. Throughout the twentieth century, Spain had fought to maintain control of its colony in Morocco (often losing badly to local forces). As a commander in Morocco, Franco was more successful than his predecessors and managed to inspire fear and even admiration in his enemies. While the rebels claimed to be fighting for a purely Catholic Spain, Franco brought over Muslim soldiers from Morocco to aid his troops. Thus the seventy to eighty thousand Moroccans were helping their conqueror create a nation in which they would be ruled as subjects and have no independence. They were well trained and effective fighters.

GERMANY—Hitler sent five thousand men, including the air force's Condor Legion, to support Franco. The Condor Legion conducted some of the most devastating bombing attacks in the war, including the destruction of Guernica.

ITALY—Mussolini sent approximately seventy thousand men to fight in Spain.

PORTUGAL—Spain's neighbor was ruled by conservatives who favored Franco. Some twenty thousand Portuguese were sent to support the fight against the Republic.

IRELAND—Eoin O'Duffy, an Irish fascist, organized a group of seven hundred men to come to Spain to fight. Some shared O'Duffy's politics; others believed they were defending the Catholic Church.

OTHERS—Tiny numbers of White Russians (Russians who had fought against the Soviets in the 1917 revolution) and fascists from France, Romania, and England, as well as at least one from the United States, came to Spain to side with Franco. They had no influence on the outcome of the war. However, some Franco supporters did influence public views of the conflict through their positions as titled English aristocrats or as writers for Catholic publications in England and the United States. A few women also came to do the same kind of nursing and family support for Franco as women on the left did for the Republic.

TIME LINE

1929		Stock market crashes
1930		Nazis win 18.3 percent of German vote, up from 2.6 percent in 1928
1931		King Alfonso XIII abdicates; Spain becomes a republic; reforms begin
1932		Japan occupies Manchuria
		Famine, created by Stalin's policies, begins in Ukraine; between six million and seven million will die
		Nazi Party wins 37.3 percent of July vote, largest total by any party in Germany
		Communist Party runs James Ford as its U.S. vice presidential candidate, the first African American to be nominated
		Franklin Delano Roosevelt is elected president of the United States
1933		Hitler is appointed chancellor of Germany
	JANUARY	André Friedmann flees Berlin; Gerta Pohorylle leaves Leipzig for Paris
	NOVEMBER	Conservatives win Spanish elections, end reforms
1934	FALL	André and Gerta meet in Paris
	OCTOBER	Strike by miners in Spain is crushed by government
	DECEMBER	An international conference of fascists meets in Switzerland, drawing representatives from seventeen countries
		There are 1,856 work stoppages in the United States, the most since World War I
1935	MAY	Despite 24 African Americans lynched in 1933 and 15 lynched in 1934, the U.S. Senate blocks anti-lynching bill; 18 African Americans will be lynched by the end of 1935

1935	SUMMER	Communist Party in the United States suggests Popular Front alliance with the Socialist Party; socialists decline
		André and Gerta fall in love
	SEPTEMBER	SEPT. 30: POUM is founded in Spain
	OCTOBER	OCT. 3: Italy invades Ethiopia
1936	FEBRUARY	Popular Front is elected in Spain
		André becomes Robert Capa; Gerta becomes Gerda Taro
	SPRING	Chim leaves France to report on the new government in Spain
		Capa photographs the Popular Front campaign in France
	MAY	Popular Front elected in France
	JULY	JULY 17: Generals begin revolt against Spanish government
		JULY 19: Madrid and Barcelona defeat forces allied with rebel generals
		Capa and Taro fly to Spain
		Trials, false confessions, and executions of former Soviet leaders begin
		France decides on nonintervention policy in Spain
	AUGUST	AUG. 14: Rebel forces capture Badajoz and massacre eighteen hundred people
		AUG. 18: Poet Federico García Lorca is arrested and subsequently murdered
		AUG. 19: Britain makes sending arms to Spain illegal

1936		
	SEPTEMBER	Capa photographs *The Falling Soldier*
		<u>SEPT. 27:</u> General Francisco Franco's forces end loyalist siege of the Alcázar in Toledo
	OCTOBER	Stalin sends arms and advisers to Spain
		<u>OCT. 25:</u> Spanish gold is shipped to Soviet Union
		International Brigades begin training in Spain
	NOVEMBER	<u>NOV. 6:</u> Spanish government moves from Madrid to Valencia
		<u>NOV. 7:</u> Battle for Madrid begins
		<u>NOV. 8:</u> International Brigades arrive in Madrid
		<u>NOV. 15:</u> German Condor Legion starts flying missions in Spain
		<u>NOV. 18:</u> Capa arrives in Madrid
		<u>NOV. 23:</u> Franco ends attack on Madrid
	DECEMBER	Communists begin push to remove POUM from power in the Catalan government of Barcelona
		Italian soldiers land in Spain
1937	FEBRUARY	<u>FEB. 6:</u> Franco attacks in the Jarama valley; International Brigades fight back
		<u>FEB. 7:</u> Málaga is attacked and falls
		Capa and Taro are back in Spain, head to Málaga
		Chim documents the Basque country
		Capa and Taro return to Madrid
	MARCH	Taro is on her own in Spain
		<u>MAR. 18:</u> Loyalists bomb Italian forces near Brihuega, forcing their retreat
	APRIL	<u>APR. 26:</u> Guernica is bombed by Condor Legion
	MAY	<u>MAY 1:</u> United States makes sending arms to Spain illegal
		Capa goes to Bilbao; Taro heads to Valencia
		<u>MAY 3—6:</u> POUM and communists fight over telephone exchange in Barcelona

1937		
		<u>MAY 25:</u> After a three-week delay, International Exposition opens in Paris; only the German and Soviet pavilions are ready in time for originally scheduled opening
	JUNE	POUM is declared illegal, and arrests begin
		Capa and Taro photograph the Segovia and Córdoba fronts
		<u>JUNE 19:</u> Bilbao falls
		Picasso completes *Guernica*; painting is installed at Spanish pavilion in Paris
	JULY	<u>JULY 4:</u> International Congress of Writers in Defense of Culture opens in Valencia; Capa and Taro cover it
		Capa returns to Paris; Taro remains
		<u>JULY 5:</u> Congress of Writers moves to Madrid
		<u>JULY 6:</u> Battle of Brunete begins; Oliver Law leads troops, then is killed
		<u>JULY 7:</u> Japan invades China
		<u>JULY 14:</u> Taro goes to Paris for a brief trip, then returns to photograph Brunete
		<u>JULY 25:</u> Taro is run over by loyalist tank, dies next day
	AUGUST	<u>AUG. 24:</u> Loyalists begin attack on Franco's forces in Aragon
	OCTOBER	<u>OCT. 28:</u> Spanish government moves from Valencia to Barcelona
	DECEMBER	Capa covers the Battle of Teruel
1938	JANUARY	<u>JAN. 8:</u> Loyalist forces capture rebel garrison in Teruel
		<u>JAN. 21:</u> Capa sails for China
	FEBRUARY	<u>FEB. 22:</u> Rebels retake Teruel
	MARCH	<u>MAR. 12:</u> Germans "annex" Austria
		<u>MAR. 16—18:</u> Italian aircraft bomb Barcelona
	JULY	<u>JULY 26:</u> Battle of the Ebro begins
	SEPTEMBER	<u>SEPT. 22:</u> Capa returns to Paris

1938	SEPTEMBER	SEPT. 30: Munich Agreement gives Hitler control over part of Czechoslovakia
	OCTOBER	OCT. 25: Capa and Chim photograph the farewell to the International Brigades
	NOVEMBER	Capa photographs the Battle of the Ebro, travels with Hemingway and other journalists
		NOV. 16: Government forces retreat from the Ebro
	DECEMBER	DEC. 23: Franco's forces begin attack on Catalonia
1939	JANUARY	Capa photographs Barcelona and massive exodus of refugees
		JAN. 20–26: Franco bombs Barcelona, and his forces enter the city
	MARCH	MAR. 28: Franco's forces enter Madrid
		Capa photographs temporary refugee camps on the beaches in France
	APRIL	APR. 1: Franco wins; the United States joins Britain and France in recognizing Franco as leader of Spain
	MAY	Chim leaves Europe on assignment to Mexico
	AUGUST	AUG. 23: Nazi-Soviet nonaggression pact is signed
	SEPTEMBER	SEPT. 1: Hitler invades Poland; World War II begins
		SEPT. 19: Capa files for a visa to the United States through Chile
	OCTOBER	OCT. 15: Capa sails for the United States
1940		Hitler invades countries across Europe, including France
1941	JUNE	JUNE 22: Germans break nonaggression pact, invade Soviet Union
	DECEMBER	DEC. 7: Japanese bomb Pearl Harbor; United States enters war
1942	JANUARY	JAN. 20: Nazis implement "Final Solution," the extermination of Jews across Europe

1943	SEPTEMBER	SEPT. 3: Allies invade Italy
1944	JUNE	JUNE 6: D-Day; Allies land in Normandy, France; Capa is the only photographer to land with the first wave of the invasion
1945	MAY	MAY 7: Germany surrenders
	AUGUST	AUG. 6: United States drops atomic bomb on Hiroshima, Japan; drops another three days later on Nagasaki
	SEPTEMBER	SEPT. 2: Japan formally surrenders
1946	FEBRUARY	FEB. 1: United Nations meets for the first time
1947		Magnum founded
1954	MAY	MAY 7: Vietnamese rebels defeat French at Dien Bien Phu
		MAY 25: Capa steps on land mine in Indochina, dies
1955		*The Family of Man* photography exhibit opens in New York
1975		Franco dies; Juan Carlos, grandson of Alfonso XIII, becomes king of Spain; new era of reform begins
2007		Mexican Suitcase is recovered
2010		International Center of Photography exhibits images from Mexican Suitcase
2011		Civil war begins in Syria; some scholars see echoes of the Spanish Civil War (see Appendix C)
2016		Eightieth anniversary of the Spanish Civil War
2017		Seventieth anniversary of Magnum

HOW WE CAME TO WRITE THIS BOOK

MARC

I GREW UP surrounded by stories of the Spanish Civil War. My father often took me to the Museum of Modern Art in Manhattan, where Picasso's *Guernica* occupied an entire wall. The painter would not allow it to be shown in Spain so long as Franco was alive, and I saw it many times. Each visit was a reminder of the horror of the assault on that town, the genius of the painter, and the long shadow of the lost war.

In school, the war came even closer. For many of the adults I knew, including my friends' parents and my teachers, standing against Franco and then being viewed with suspicion in America as so-called premature antifascists were vivid experiences. Indeed, my high school math teacher, Sol Birnbaum, had been a proud member of the Abraham Lincoln Brigade. We all knew that and admired him for it. Sol was a short but fit man who sported a black beret, perhaps a fashion statement from his days overseas. His view of the world was shaped in Spain, and he had done research that our government wanted but that he refused to share, since he did not agree with its policies.

In tenth grade, our Spanish teacher was a beautiful young Spanish woman who wore black leather boots. For all the boys, she symbolized the dark intensity of her homeland. And then the following year, with a new teacher, we began to read the works of Federico García Lorca. I fell in love with his haunting, passionate dreams-in-words. I cannot say strongly enough what a treasure he is—try the "Lament for Ignacio Sánchez Mejías" or "Romance Sonambulo." At least view one of the many YouTube videos. But there is the greatest joy in speaking—and even memorizing—his resonant Spanish words that are both aching love and heart-stopping nightmare.

Spain and its civil war were about passion, death, tragedy, loss—and near at hand. *For Whom the Bell Tolls* was a book I was pleased to read in order to be part of the adult conversation. But I also read and loved books by John Dos Passos. (*Nineteen Nineteen* is a treat!) As I got older, I began to hear the stories of the fate of his translator, and of how Stalin subverted and infiltrated the Left. The whole tragedy of Spain began to seem like a myth I had too eagerly accepted. It was the story a generation before me told, full of their nostalgia, their regret. It was as if I had grown up wearing old clothes, and I now realized I could take them off, could choose my own fashion. Spain was their fight; it did not mean anything to me.

Working on *Eyes of the World*, though, changed the story for me once again. Rereading Hemingway and Orwell—and for the first time the Spanish Civil War writings of authors such as Langston Hughes, Josephine Herbst, Gustav Regler, and Alvah Bessie—and looking at the photos with Marina, I felt for the first time, for myself, what Spain had meant. I didn't have to squint and ignore Stalin—I veered off to study the history of his murders (which included members of my family) in detail. But I discovered the feeling we tried to capture in this book: the "thrill of hope" Orwell described, that sense of being young, having no past, no home, nothing to lose, and a vision of doing right, fighting evil, the desperate need to build a better future. Spain was, for a moment, hope, an ideal, a place where young people could plant their dreams.

Today we read dystopian novels and perhaps fight for environmental, social, or economic causes. We, too, have our dreams. May Spain guide us—not just to prepare for the challenges, and even defeats, ahead, but to recall the force, the power, of its yearning. The Republic fell to Franco and his long dictatorship. But he, too, passed. The multiracial ideals of the international utopians are now our commonplace reality. Dreams matter.

MARINA: "THE MAIL SLOT"

WHEN I WAS A LITTLE GIRL, I would wait eagerly for the mail to arrive, listening for the *thunk* of envelopes and magazines dropping through the brass slot into our foyer. What I waited for most was *Life* magazine.

Then I would lie belly down on the living room rug and slowly, slowly make my way through the magazine, start to finish. I loved the ripple of its oversized pages, the oily scent of ink. Most of all, I loved how a news story rolled out before me, photo after photo, in a muscular wave. First I would let the images flow all at once, riffling past in a sequence, like a film. Then I would go back, pause, pore over a single image, study its details. Some photographs walloped me so hard, I came to a trembling stop.

That's what happened when I saw the first photos taken right after Martin Luther King Jr. was shot on a motel balcony in April 1968. I had already heard the news, of course, on the television. But my brain kept seizing up, trying to make sense of the astonishing fact that Dr. King, the round-faced man whom so many adults adored and admired, was dead. I was looking at a picture taken the instant after he had been shot. The picture showed his aides, pointing at a window across the motel courtyard. Death caught and stilled. How could I, a little girl, be let in on this momentous event? It seemed both obscene and right.

Other images scared me, especially those from Vietnam: the Buddhist monk who burned himself; the naked girl running down a road, arms outstretched, seared by napalm; helicopters tilting out of burning villages; the sinister stillness of the Mekong River; the college student on her knees at Kent State, a friend sprawled dead on the ground.

As I grew up in the 1960s and 1970s, the world was rushing in, stirring me deeper into America's shimmering, urgent events. The Vietnam War, civil rights, integration battles, assassinations, the breakdown of New York City, the feminist movement, all surged around us and blared in headlines and on the television. These events were like electricity zapping in the air, debated nightly at dinner tables, out on porches, at neighborhood gatherings and parties. But I was young; it was my brother's friends who were of draft age and marched against the war; it was my father who went off to teach in public schools beset with bomb threats and protests. I did not understand all this fully. Photographs helped me make sense of the rush of news that breached my home and overwhelmed me.

News was part of my everyday fare. I woke up every morning hearing the *snap-snap* sound of my mother turning the pages of the *New York Times* as she read. By third grade, my teacher, Miss Citrin, told us that we must read one article a week and write up a report for Friday current events. I pasted my *New York Times* articles in my blue loose-leaf binder—thin strips of news about the Cold War, the Soviet Union, or protests at local city colleges. To this day, I cannot wake up and feel my brain's muscles go into motion without reading the newspaper.

Photos, though, were different; they rearranged something vital inside me. They transformed the flat, noisy headlines, the epic political events that were heaving across our globe, and made them understandable. For a little girl, they turned the big and frightening into the intimate. There was safety in going toward those stills, taking in each image at my own pace, thumb and forefinger on the page's edge. In a strange way, those photo spreads gave me control: page by page, I could let out the throttle of fear, just so, before taking in the next image.

There is something both private and public in a news photo; it is an exchange between you and figures and events that are remote—the unknown soldier who is wounded on a battlefield, or Coretta Scott King at Dr. King's funeral, veil covering her eyes. You are being let in on a private, unguarded moment that is also shared by millions. I stared at Coretta Scott King's daughter, her face scrunched up into her mother's chest, and saw a girl like me. Her neat ribbons and carefully parted hair, her stiff white dress. That terrible event came down to my size. I was allowed *in*.

I did not know then that as I paged through *Life* magazine, I was absorbing a way of seeing invented by a small band of young photographers decades before, during the Spanish Civil War. Photography was their calling, fusing with the ideals and fervor of their times. It was their legacy that shaped me. At some point, I became aware of Magnum and those original images from Spain, but it is not an exact memory. It's as if they were always there: the classic faces, the strong, molding light. They were a foundation of seeing. In the magazines of my childhood—*Life*, *Look*, *National Geographic*, *The Family of Man* catalog—I was seeing versions of Capa and Taro and Chim everywhere.

I realize that in an age of digital manipulation, Instagram, Pinterest, Facebook feeds, and avant-garde photo installations, my ideas of photography might seem a little old fashioned. In fact, there are photographers who rebelled against Magnum and the photojournalism tradition, calling it "pious humanism." They did not believe that a photograph could teach or change the world. But for me, strong images never lose their power.

Writing the story of Capa and Taro was like going back to my origins. And yet their story was more heartbreaking, more moving and urgent than I ever realized. Each tour through the photographs, each detail in the ups and downs of their survival, each example of their sheer bravery, brought me fresh amazement and grief. I know I can never be as courageous and reckless as Capa and Taro, or any of the other great photographers who have followed. Seeing their photos, I can only be grateful for their willingness to put themselves on the line in pursuit of the story, of the right image. For letting me travel with them, to see all that happened. Capa, Taro, and their friend Chim were optimistic; they were fearless and canny—and they were most of all young, oh so young. And they brought to me—a little girl growing up decades later—a way to see and understand my complicated, difficult world.

COLLABORATION

ONE OF THE REASONS we wanted to write about Capa and Taro is because they were an artistic couple who worked together as equals. Of course, we are also a couple, are both writers, and have a lot of experience in collaborating. At several points in the book, we envisioned how they experienced that creative exchange. Where do those passages come from? Research, photos, and our own experience.

Neither Capa nor Taro left self-reflective diaries, and only a few of their letters have survived. We are left with how others saw them, the chronology of their relationship and work life, and their photos. Every researcher interested in Capa and Taro tries to make sense of each beat of their relationship. What did *copain* mean to her? To him? Was she pulling away at the end? If so, was that because she so valued her independence that, even if she loved him, she needed marriage to come later, when she would not be in his shadow? Was she more committed to the Left, and he to photography? Later Capa did become a ladies' man; even the Hollywood beauty Ingrid Bergman could not get him to settle down. Was that because he was heartbroken over Taro? Or did Taro sense that he would stray, and so she refused to attach? We have made use of others' ideas, especially Irme Schaber's deep research on these questions. But ultimately our interest is less in the unknowable shifts in their relationship than in their experience as artistic partners. And to understand that, we ventured to speculate based on our own experiences.

What is collaboration? What are the challenges, the rewards? What makes it work?

MARC

I WAS, YOU MIGHT SAY, the product of artistic collaboration. My father, Boris, was a well-established New York set designer. Theater work, especially for a set designer, is inherently collaborative. Designing a stage set is not making a poster; it is creating a space that comes alive when it is used. My mother's part in this process involved not just designs but people.

My mother, Lisa, had grown up in Europe, where her father was a musical conductor. The composers with whom he worked were the experimental modernists Arnold Schoenberg, Anton Webern, and Alban Berg. They were each ferociously talented, but equally competitive and self-assertive. My grandfather had the gift of wit and charm and managed to smooth the way among them.

My mother grew up surrounded by discussions and rehearsals in and around whatever apartment they occupied. She studied scenic design and, in America, became my father's assistant. Before they were a couple, they were artists together—sort of. In Playbills, my father always received sole billing, with my mother hidden on one of the last pages, listed under her maiden name as Mr. Aronson's assistant. But every director, producer, and actor knew that they were partners—not only in crafting scenic designs (she built many of the models) but in doing what her own father had done: negotiating the mammoth egos of the theater world (my father's included) to allow the individual stars to function as a creative team.

My parents worked at home; their studio was the front room of our Upper West Side apartment. Work went on in one form or another all the time, every day of the year. There were clashes between my parents, and friction with visiting guests. I heard the sharp edges of artistic firefights. I saw famous directors, actors, producers, and authors sit together—argue, show off, and dispute, but also sparkle, challenge, and inspire one another. And I saw designs take shape—from a sketch my father might make late at night, to a small model my mother built, to a larger model crafted by an assistant, to a meeting with a director about revisions, to the scenic studio where drawings became drops and models turned into buildings, to a stage where my parents' images became a world brought to life in a play.

I began my own career in book publishing as an editor: the most collaborative job. In one way, an editor is there to assist an author or artist, to help that creator be his or her best. In another, the editor stands between the creators and the publishing house, which has its own social anthropology, its own layers of power, status, hierarchy, as well as its own governing requirements, such as deadlines, cost, and income. I love editing, but I am also now an author. And as an author, I have shared the writing process on seven of my books. Even Marina and I were initially author and editor on one previous Holt book (Marina's *Remix: Conversations with Immigrant Teenagers.*) From art to marriage—like my parents.

I think collaboration comes down to two essentials. First, honesty. When any of us works in a group, there is a get-along–go-along, you-scratch-my-back–I'll-scratch-yours impulse. If I don't criticize you too much—which becomes especially appealing when you work with someone you live with—you won't be too hard on me. Harsh criticism can carry a real emotional price. But you must be committed to what you are creating. The something that you are bringing into the world together must be larger than your fear, your ego, your momentary peace. You must care most about the goal: making your art the best it can be. Anything you choose to ignore may very well be exactly what others will notice. Your obligation is to creation, not calm. Of course, this also means you have to be able to listen and adjust to apt criticism of your own work.

The second essential might seem like the opposite of the first, for it is the ability to fall in love, to be swept away by what your partner has created. You must be a fan, an enthusiast, an encourager who can swoon over a decision that replaces something ordinary with something inspired. You cannot be rigid; you have to be mobile when your partner leads beyond what you could create on your own.

When an artistic relationship has honesty and mutual passion, you together can craft works that are new, that give the world depth, beauty, insight. That birth is so rewarding, so satisfying, so fundamentally true—even as one is said to "true" a plank of wood, or a bicycle wheel—that all the aggravation disappears. You delight in each other, and in your art.

In speculating about several moments when Capa and Taro worked together, shot together, traveled together, we tried to imagine and describe that experience of delight.

MARINA: "COULD"

WHEN I WAS IN MY TWENTIES, I spent a lot of time alone. At that time, I was in graduate school, living a Spartan existence, all my energy fused to learning the craft of writing. I felt so guilty about quitting my salaried job that I told myself I must treat writing like a job. I lived in a tiny studio apartment and sat at my small table and wrote, every day. I was fierce about my solitude.

Just beyond my elbow, through the window, lay the driveway of a big Victorian house where a young couple and their children lived. Every day, while I made coffee and sat down to write, I could hear the messy tumble of family life, voices shouting, their Subaru backing into the street. I hardened my heart and pressed into the page. That life—marriage, work, children—seemed impossible for me.

By the time I emerged a few years later, I wondered whether marriage would force me to leave that most central passion, the one that animated me and got me up every day. My ideal literary couple was Virginia and Leonard Woolf—I loved how they had created Hogarth Press together, how he nursed her through her difficulties as an artist.

One day, I came upon a quote in a memoir of the American author Mary McCarthy. She wrote of her marriage to the critic Edmund Wilson, which, by all accounts, wasn't very good, mostly because he drank too much. But she still wrote appreciatively of why she had decided to marry him: that he cared not for what she was but what she could be. That idea—*what she could be*—lodged in me like a hot coal. *That's what I must find in a partner.*

So often when we think of romance or dating, we hope we look good and put on our best face. But in a way, finding a partner is not about who you are now. It's finding someone who can see your potential—even if it's not totally apparent to you. A partnership is not about the present but the future. All the *coulds*—what you could do on your own and together—begin to shimmer as real possibilities.

When I met Marc, we would take long walks in our beloved New York City, talking about writing and books and history. One evening we were having dinner at one of our favorite restaurants when Marc remarked, "You're really smart in the way you talk about fiction." I felt a sudden warmth in my chest. It was like a tiny flame turning on. A part of myself that felt hidden became visible. Marc's easy sense of collaboration, his family's history, was a revelation. He softened the fierce borders I had created around myself. I finally graduated from my tiny studio apartment to that large rambling house on the other side of the driveway, with its noise and chaos and expansiveness.

This was the essence of Capa and Taro's relationship: they recognized in each other what they *could* be. When Gerta met André, he was a disheveled, charming, not-very-serious photographer. But Gerta saw in André Friedmann a tremendous talent. He, in turn, was not threatened when she wanted to take up photography; he encouraged her interest. They weren't focused on what they were—penniless, unknown—but what they could be. They invented their future selves.

People often ask, Does working on a book together ruin your marriage? We are always puzzled by this. Working on a book together, or sharing a project we are separately working on, *is* our marriage. It's all the *could*s we are making happen. It's no different from making sure dinner is on the table and our boys are happy. When Marc was writing *Sir Walter Ralegh and the Quest for El Dorado*, I sat with Marc and made him write and rewrite certain scenes while our infant son napped or played in the playpen. Vacations as a family quickly became working holidays. We sat across from each other, sharing pages, talking through what we were writing or what was next. Now that our boys are older, we include them in the process, too—asking them questions, or giving them pages, or having them join in on research and field trips.

The greatest gift collaboration gives you is a feeling that something nearly hidden can exist. The *could*—that tiny, flickering flame hidden in you—becomes visible. In sharing it with your collaborator, your *copain*, it is now on the outside. A gust grows, builds within you. Your idea takes shape. Now it grows in new ways. All because you have this friend, this fellow seeker who believes that what was once phantom can become solid and real.

This is what Capa and Taro gave each other. After Taro's death, Capa never again had a romantic relationship that mingled love and work. From then on, he kept the two separate. Yet even as Capa became the "greatest war-photographer," even as he turned into a roving ladies' man who would never settle down, even as Taro's reputation was overshadowed by his later fame and by politics, this early collaboration remains. It was a time when they were at their most vulnerable and, thus, most open to changing who they were. They invented each other. They understood the power of the *could*. And they changed the way all of us could see.

ACKNOWLEDGMENTS

WE HAVE BEEN TRULY FORTUNATE in that so many people who are experts in their fields were generous with their time, their insights, and their assistance. Every decision in this book, however, was ours and is our responsibility; in honoring those who helped us, we in no sense imply that they made our choices.

This book exists only because Cynthia Young and the International Center for Photography helped us find nearly all of the images, located every letter and interview we needed, read and reread the text, and reviewed the photos and layout. Claartje van Dijk stood by us in the old archive building, seeking out ever more resources and answering countless e-mails thereafter. While ICP was our editorial guide and provided links where Magnum did not hold a particular image, Magnum Photos—through the good offices of Michael Shulman—became our true partner. They agreed to give us limitless access in return for a share of our earnings. Without ICP and Magnum, this book would simply not be possible.

Decades ago, in junior high, Lisa Berger and Marina used to help their Spanish teacher after class. Lisa went on to be fluent in both Spanish and Catalan and has made her own powerful documentaries related to the Spanish Civil War. When we traveled to Spain to follow in our photographers' footsteps, it was she who provided entrée, setting up contacts, sharing her research, and later navigating the mysteries of Spanish rights, rules, and regulations on our behalf.

Alan Warren was a wonderfully informed guide in Barcelona, along the Ebro (where our sons found cartridges from the war still scattered on the ground), and in Les Masies—where Capa photographed the disbandment of the International Brigades. Ernesto Vinas was a similarly insightful guide to the battle of Brunete. Alan led us to Angela Jackson, who has pioneered the study of British women and the Spanish Civil War. The true scholars who have done pathbreaking research on our photographers include: Irme Schaber on Gerda Taro, Carole Naggar on Chim, and again Cynthia Young on Capa. All three were constantly available to answer questions or offer insights, as was Ben Schneiderman (Chim's nephew) and Peter Stein (Fred Stein's son). Thanks to both for letting us use their relatives' photos. Amanda Vaill, who has done her own original research into the sources for her excellent book on three couples at the Hotel Florida during the conflict, was an enthusiastic, generous supporter from the first moment she heard of our project. Dr. Judith Keene read an early version of the manuscript and brought us both her deep knowledge of the conflict in Spain and again most welcome encouragement. Dr. Juan Salas, whom we met fortuitously, gave us more valuable leads on photography and the war.

Thanks to the government of Spain for making images available to us. The Trabajadores site at the University of Warwick is a marvel, and Carole Jones there helped us track down everything we wanted to see. Lynda Claassen at the Southworth Collection of the University of California San Diego and Chloe Morse-Harding at Brandeis University were also of great help in our image research. Kirin and Sunaya DasGupta Mueller translated an important letter from German. Amanda Viehmeyer and Brian Giles plowed through our piles of books to help organize our notes and bibliography. Norman Cowie and Kerry Dubyk were last-minute saviors.

Sally Doherty at Holt understood this vast project from the first, kept her gimlet eye on every word, and guided it through the house, and Rachel Murray took on innumerable tasks to facilitate the process; April Ward was truly brilliant as a designer—seeing the essence of the image and text flow. Jennifer Healey was a model of a managing editor in handling a cascade of details. Gail Hochman found us the right house, and Erin Cox—Marc's agent and a publicist in her own right—is helping us bring the book to the world.

Sasha and Rafi have grown up watching this book take shape around them. We hope that at least some of the time they found that an inspiration rather than a distraction from our family life.

SOURCES

THE RESEARCH FOR THIS BOOK involved three distinct sets of materials: the history of the Spanish Civil War; the history of photography; and the biographies of Capa, Taro, and Chim. Here is a basic road map to the layers of scholarship and controversy we encountered in our research. We hope this guide is useful to anyone who wants to read further on these subjects.

From the moment the Spanish Civil War ended, historians began arguing over the story of what happened. You can get a sense of how intense these fights have been by looking at the first three appendices: whether it is a photo or a death in battle, every aspect of the war has inspired raging partisanship and controversy. For those who want to get oriented, there is a fine essay by George Esenwein in his source book *The Spanish Civil War: A Modern Tragedy*.

Reading the essay is like perusing a travel guide before going on a trip to an intriguing but unfamiliar land. Because the Republic lost, several essential questions run through books on the war: (1) Could the Republic have won? How? (2) If it did, what kind of Spain would that have been? (3) Could Hitler have been stopped earlier and the devastations of World War II prevented? (4) Were those who went to Spain to fight for the Republic farseeing heroes or shortsighted dupes of the Soviet Union? While historians debate these issues through detailed research, the story of the war came to the general reading public through memoirs and novels that, on the whole, treat the war as a heroic lost cause. There was often a rather male slant to these memoirs, focusing on combat and male camaraderie with sensual and sidelined women.

Here is a short version of Esenwein's essay: Franco wanted only his side glorified, while those who fought for the Republic had the opposite aim. Following pathbreaking work by the British historian Hugh Thomas, scholars began to move past those split positions. Then a new front opened when Burnett Bolloten explored the divide between the two sides within the Left—those who wanted a social revolution right away and those in government who were more cautious and were strongly influenced by the Soviets. Was the Republic doomed by its own inner conflict? After the fall of the Soviet Union, a new wave of scholars shifted the focus to the machinations and calculations of the Soviets. Had Franco been defeated, this set of scholars suggested, Spain would have become something like the states in Eastern Europe that the Soviets dominated between 1945 and 1989. Perhaps, then, it is a good thing the Republic lost. Yet another set of primarily British scholars, such as Helen Graham and Paul Preston, rejected this idea and defended a more positive image of the Republican cause. That debate continues today.

Cultural historians have examined the artwork created during the war—the propaganda war both inside and outside of Spain. More recently, attention has shifted from the overarching issues to the roles of women in combat and as writers and nurses. And a senior scholar has looked once again at Franco to reevaluate him. In turn, books for the general public, such as Richard Rhodes's *Hell and Good Company*, explore new angles such as the innovations in blood transfusions during the war and no longer assume that readers strongly identify with one side or another. As we reviewed the proofs of this book, Adam Hochschild's *Spain in Our Hearts: Americans in the Spanish Civil War 1936–1939* was published. This is the best current book on the war from an American pro-Left but fair-minded point of view. He builds the book around personal stories, and it is rich with evocative anecdotes, a few of which we were able to weave into captions. Mr. Hochschild was kind enough to read our book in galleys.

The first person to tell the story of Robert Capa, and to build the legend, was Capa himself. With his characteristic charm, he titled his sort-of memoir *Slightly Out of Focus*. From the title on, he was saying that this was not exactly true in all respects. The many memoirs and books on the Spanish Civil War published in the 1950s and 1960s often included mentions of Capa, and less frequently Taro. Unfortunately, as in Peter Wyden's *The Passionate War* and more recently Alex Kershaw's *Blood and Champagne: The Life and Times of Robert Capa*, the tone was often macho appreciation of Capa and skepticism or worse about Taro. In Capa's lifetime, this eclipsing of Taro was, in part, a result of the McCarthyite mood of the early 1950s, when their association with the Left and Soviet communism was downplayed. But for the very same reason, in European countries with strong Communist Parties or actually under Soviet domination, Taro was revered as a martyr—a modern Joan of Arc—but for her politics more than her photography.

Richard Whelan devoted his career to thoroughly researching Capa's life and, along the way, came to a greater appreciation and understanding of Taro. The actual interviews he did to create his work are available at the ICP and were the most rewarding resource for us.

The discovery of the Mexican Suitcase and the fall of Soviet communism began a shift. Scholars of photography were able to confirm the work on Capa and Taro that Whelan and Irme Schaber had begun. Schaber's careful research really created the field of Taro scholarship but, unfortunately, was never translated into English. We had to make our way through French and German versions, a YouTube video of a presentation Schaber gave at the Frontline Club in London, as well as Schaber's generous responses to our e-mails. Chim's life and work were traced by Carole Naggar.

Most recently, as in Amanda Vaill's lively and thoroughly researched *Hotel Florida*, writers have begun looking at Capa and Taro. Vaill was extremely generous and helpful in sharing insights and sources with us. The renewed appreciation of Taro as an artist, and as part of the Capa-Taro team, is similar to the shift among historians away from old ideological fights and toward an awareness of what the war meant for women and for the interaction between men and women.

One of the fascinating aspects of researching this book was examining the history of photography in magazines and advertisements. The innovations in layout in French far Left publications such as *Vu*, *Regards*, and *Ce Soir* were brought to America by people including Capa's mentor, André Kertész, and Alexander Liberman, who became a supremely influential editorial director at *Vogue* and other Condé Nast publications (for example of Liberman's *Vu* covers, see pages 11, 68, and 100). Art styles that were originally featured alongside anticapitalist political causes found a home in fashion magazines, advertisements, and even movies such as *An American in Paris*. Those interested in Liberman should read *Them*, a memoir of Alexander and his wife, Tatiana, by their daughter, the prominent author Francine du Plessix Gray.

IMAGE CREDITS

All photographs by Robert Capa on the following pages are copyright Robert Capa © International Center of Photography/Magnum Photos: ii (right), x, 2, 3, 5, 6, 8 (photo of Capa), 9, 12 (photo of Capa), 13 (Capa ID), 21 (both), 24, 26, 27, 28, 30, 31, 32, 33, 35, 36, 37 (both), 38, 39, 51, 52, 53 (left), 55, 56, 59, 63, 65, 67, 82, 84, 85, 87, 89, 90, 91, 92, 94 (both), 95, 108, 113 (left), 115, 116, 117, 119, 132, 136, 144, 146, 147, 148, 149, 150, 177, 180, 196, 202, 207 (both), 208, 210, 211, 212, 213, 214, 215 (left), 218 (photo of Capa), 220, 221 (both), 222 (both), 223, 225, 226 (photo of Capa), 227, 229, 230 (photo of Capa), 231, 232, 236 (photo of Capa), 243, 245.

All photographs by Gerda Taro on the following pages are copyright Gerda Taro © International Center of Photography: ii-iii (left and background), 15 (photo of Taro), 46, 47 (both), 48, 49, 53 (right), 57, 58, 62, 111, 113 (right), 120 (photo of Taro), 123, 124, 125, 127, 128, 151, 152 (left), 154, 156, 157, 158, 159, 160, 161, 162, 165, 168, 171, 172, 173, 178, 182, 184, 185, 186 (both), 187, 188 (both), 189, 190, 193.

All photographs by Chim (David Seymour) on the following pages are copyright © Estate of Chim (David Seymour)/Magnum Photos: 61, 81, 93, 104, 139, 176, 228, 241 (left).

All photographs by Henri Cartier-Bresson on these pages are copyright © Henri Cartier-Bresson/Magnum Photos: 234, 241 (right).

The following photos are courtesy Collection Capa/Magnum Photos: 230, Michel Descamps (Paris Match); 236, Ruth Orkin.

The book and magazine covers and spreads on the following pages are courtesy of the International Center of Photography, Collection International Center of Photography: 11, 23, 44, 68, 71, 96, 97, 98, 100, 103, 105, 106, 107, 129, 130, 141, 152 (right), 166, 169, 199, 204, 205, 209, 215 (right).

All documents (contact notebooks, letters, telegram, and press passes) on the following pages are courtesy Collection International Center of Photography/The Robert Capa and Cornell Capa Archive: 101, 112, 118, 122, 153, 195, 200, 238.

All photographs by Fred Stein on the following pages are copyright © Estate of Fred Stein, fredstein.com: cover, 16, 18, 20.

All photographs by unidentified photographers are copyright © International Center of Photography: 17.

The materials on the following pages are from the University of Warwick Trabajadores Collection: 29, Publications from the archive of Paul Tofahrn MSS 238/PUB/4/4 17; 43, Archives of the Trades Union Congress MSS 292/808.91/41; 76 (top), Archives of the Trades Union Congress MSS292/946/18b/84; 76 (bottom), Maitland-Sara-Hallinan collection MSS 15x/1/293/1/15; 79, Publications from the archive of Henry Sara and Frank Maitland MSS 15/3/8/239; 134, Publications from the archive of Henry Sara and Frank Maitland Journal of the Friends of the Spanish Republic 15/3/8/255/12; 143, Publications from the archive of Paul Tofahrn MSS 238/PUP/4/4 27.

The image of a Leica courtesy of George Eastman Museum: 34.

The materials on the following pages are courtesy Brandeis University Spanish Civil War Poster Collection, Robert D. Farber University Archives & Special Collections Department: 80, 256 (right).

The materials on the following pages are from archives in Spain: 41, España, Ministerio de Educación, Cultura y Deporte, Centro Documental de la Memoria Histórica, Armero, Carteles, 637; 50, España, Ministerio de Educación, Cultura y Deporte, Archivo General de la Administración, Archivo Fotográfico de la Delegación de Propaganda de Madrid durante la Guerra Civil, signatura F-04048-54041 (Fotógrafo Prats); 72, España, Ministerio de Educación, Cultura y Deporte, Centro Documental de la Memoria Histórica, Armero, Carteles, 650; 170, España, Ministerio de Educación, Cultura y Deporte, Centro Documental de la Memoria Histórica, PS-Carteles, 302; 175, Museo Nacional Centro de Arte Reina Sofía (MNCARS), Ministerio de Educación, Cultura y Deporte de España; 255 (left), "El Comunismo" España, Ministerio de Educación, Cultura y Deporte, Centro Documental de la Memoria Histórica, Armero, Carteles, 694; 255 (right) "Accion Popular" España, Ministerio de Educación, Cultura y Deporte, Centro Documental de la Memoria Histórica, Armero, Carteles, 520; 256 (left), "Obreros" Fundació Josep Renau – València.

Ramón Gaya Poster © 2016 Artists Rights Society (ARS), New York / VEGAP, Madrid: 170.

Stamp courtesy Mandeville Special Collections UC San Diego Library: 179.

Public domain: 102 (appears in Schaber, Whelan, and Lubben's *Gerda Taro*, p. 27); 163 (appears in Frizot and de Veigy's *Vu*, pp. 46–47).

NOTES

PROLOGUE

1   At the top are hundreds of Nazi troops: Kershaw, *Blood and Champagne*, p. 124.

3   "We'll have only one chance": Kershaw, *Blood and Champagne*, p. 121.

3   "They are tough experienced men": Capa, in Whelan, *This Is War!*, p. 214.

4   "Exhausted from the water and the fear": Whelan, *Robert Capa: A Biography*, p. 212.

4   "The empty camera trembled in my hands": Capa, *Slightly Out of Focus*, p. 148.

5   "in the water, holding his cameras": Whelan, *This Is War!*, p. 235.

CHAPTER ONE

7   *If he could just find the girl*: The story of Capa approaching Ruth Cerf in a café to be a model for a Swiss insurance assignment is told in all the major biographies of both Capa and Taro. Details were amplified with a Whelan interview with Ruth Cerf Berg, May 2, 1982; Berg letter to Peter Wyden, Mar. 27, 1987, translated from the German by Kirin and Sunaya DasGupta Mueller.

8   "unity of mind and will": Adolf Hitler, "Appeal to the German People," Jan. 31, 1933, German History in Documents and Images, germanhistorydocs.ghi-dc.org.

9   But the United States has strict limits: see Marc Aronson, *Race: A History Beyond Black and White* (New York: Atheneum, 2007), pp. 195–200.

9   "Conditions in Paris": Robert Capa letter to his nieces, February 1935, International Center of Photography.

11   "Growing up in Budapest": interview and notes of Geza Korvin Karpathi by Josefa Stuart, ICP, no date.

11   "You are a cancer of the class!": Cornell Capa, interview and notes, ICP, no date.

12   "The girls in the [Communist] Party are too ugly": Whelan, *Robert Capa: A Biography*, p. 59.

12   "The most charming boy": interview of Fred Stein by Josefa Stuart, ICP.

14   "beautiful, like a little deer, with big eyes, auburn hair, and fine features": Henri Cartier-Bresson, interview by Josefa Stuart, Jan. 23, 1959, ICP.

15   Immediately, they fled into hiding: Schaber, Whelan, and Lubben, eds. *Gerda Taro*, p. 12.

15   bright checked skirt: Rogoyska, *Gerda Taro: Inventing Robert Capa*, p. 26.

16   On weekends, they'd stay in their room: Berg interview by Whelan, Apr. 2, 1982, ICP.

17   "we were all of the Left": Berg to Wyden, Mar. 27, 1987.

17   These images have been attributed to Fred Stein, but his son is not sure of that claim.

CHAPTER TWO

19   "in Madrid I felt I had become a nobody": Capa letter to Gerta Pohorylle, April 1935, ICP.

19–23   The details of Capa and Taro's life together in Paris are drawn largely from his letters to his mother, Julia Friedmann, in the years 1934–36, ICP.

20   "Imagine, Mother": Capa to Friedmann, Sept. 9, 1935.

20   "Considering that she is even more intelligent": Capa to Friedmann, Nov. 15, 1935.

21   "She does not put a lock on her mouth": Capa to Friedmann, Nov. 15, 1935.

21   "Ragged one": Capa to Friedmann, Apr. 8, 1936.

21   "The good girl she is," Capa to Friedmann, Feb. 5, 1936.

21   "Our money momentarily": Capa to Friedmann, September 1935, ICP.

22   "Never before in my life have I been so happy!": Whelan, *Robert Capa: A Biography*, p. 74.

23 "One could almost say that I've been born again": Whelan, *Robert Capa: A Biography*, p. 80.

23 "a farewell to any fixed point": Maspero, *Out of the Shadows*, p. 39.

CHAPTER THREE

25 "At the very moment": Joseph Freeman in Marc Aronson, *Master of Deceit: J. Edgar Hoover and America in the Age of Lies* (Somerville, MA: Candlewick), p. 66.

27 The twentieth century: Benito Mussolini, *The Doctrine of Fascism*, 1932, text available at worldfuturefund.org.

29 Every weekend brings another Popular Front march: Whelan, *Robert Capa: A Biography*, p. 84.

31 "Chim thought about everything very deeply": Henri Cartier-Bresson, interview by Richard Whelan, Apr. 13, 1982, ICP.

32 "crouching and watching like a cat": Fred Stein, interview by Richard Whelan, ICP, no date.

37 "Call yourself a photojournalist": Whelan, *Robert Capa: A Biography*, p. 58.

37 "It was a job immigrants": Michel Lefebvre and Bernard Lebrun, "Where Does the Mexican Suitcase Come From?" in *The Mexican Suitcase*, ed. Cynthia Young, Vol. 1, p.75.

39 "Tell that ridiculous boy Friedmann": Whelan, *Robert Capa: A Biography*, p. 88.

39 By the time they return to the house: Interview with Josefa Stuart, in Vaill, *Hotel Florida*, p. 32.

40 "Everyone in his senses knew": Burnett Bolloten, *The Grand Camouflage: The Communist Conspiracy in the Spanish Civil War* (New York: Frederick A. Praeger, 1961), p. 18.

40 "At stake": Vaill, *Hotel Florida*, p. 1.

40–41 "Long live the Popular Front!": Dolores Ibárruri, speech July 19, 1936, Madrid, translated by Fabien Malouin, available on "No Pasaran," Wikisource, http://en.wikisource.org/wiki.

42 In Madrid, restaurants serve free meals: Thomas, *The Spanish Civil War*, p. 292.

42 "When the fighting broke out": Orwell, *Homage to Catalonia*, p. 48.

42 "Dear boy": Chim, letter to a friend, Jan. 29, 1932, Chim Archive, courtesy of Ben Schneiderman.

43 "they were deeply in love": Lebrun and Lefebvre, *Robert Capa: The Paris Years*, p. 86.

43 "far beyond the trenches of Madrid": Mikhail Koltsov in Schlögel, *Moscow, 1937*, pp. 95–96. Schlögel is quoting from another book that is largely drawn from Koltsov's writing for *Pravda*.

43 "This world will not be worth living": Matthews, *Two Wars and More to Come*, p. 207.

CHAPTER FOUR

47 Barcelona is "startling and overwhelming": Orwell, p. 4.

48 "When we went into the villages": Lisa Berger and Carol Mazer, directors, *De toda la vida* [All our lives], 1986, 55 min., https://youtube /1-4.SVzmzW4.

49 "small but enormously strong": Berg interview by Whelan, Apr. 2, 1982.

50 "The revolutionary posters were everywhere": Orwell, p. 5.

51 "bellowing revolutionary songs all day": Orwell, p. 5.

53 Spain is often called: Sun and shade (*sol y sombra*) is certainly a cliché, and it would be easy to show how it oversimplifies Spanish history, or is equally apt for other countries. But it is the phrase that the Spanish Civil War tour guide Alan Warren used in discussing the revenge killings during the war with us, and thus we feel justified in using it here.

54 The Falangists are fierce fighters: Preston, *The Spanish Civil War*, p. 55.

54 shoot them in the cemetery: Preston, *The Spanish Civil War*, p. 55.

54 "hold him while a third," and "sick at heart": Jay Allen, *Chicago Tribune*, Aug. 30, 1936; part I, page 2.

55 "a group of peasants": Szurek, *The Shattered Dream*, p. 93.

57 "this tawny land": Jay Allen, prologue to *Death in the Making*, by Robert Capa (New York: Covici Friede, 1938).

58 During this time seventeen hundred agrarian collectives will be created: Berger and Mazer, directors, *De toda la vida* [All our lives], 1986, 55 min., https://youtube/1-4.SVzmzW4.

59 "the mingled boredom and discomfort of stationary warfare": Orwell, p. 24.

61 "I love Spain": Wyden, *The Passionate War*, p. 120.

61 The rebels and their hostages: Wyden, p. 123.

64 "They both had a way of not appearing": Herbert Matthews interview by Josefa Stuart, ICP.

64 "almost children": Vaill, pp. 55–56.

65 "like people and let them know it": Cornell Capa in Hardt, "Remembering Capa," p. 35.

CHAPTER FIVE

70   "The Strait of Gibraltar": Wyden, p. 81.

73   The gold shipment: Payne, *Fascism in Spain*, p. 150.

73   "deed or thought": Stalin in Aronson, *Master of Deceit*, p. 97; several recent academic books, including Snyder, *Bloodlands*, Schlögel, *Moscow*, and Payne, *The Spanish Civil War*, emphasize the connection between extreme repression in the Soviet Union and the propaganda value of supporting the Republic. To get a sense of life in Stalin's Russia, see M. T. Anderson, *Symphony for the City of the Dead* (Somerville, MA: Candlewick, 2015).

74   "Far below and flat to the eye lay Spain": Bessie, *Men in Battle*, p. 24.

75   "lemon-trees with their bright": Bessie, *Men in Battle*, p. 25.

75   "There has been nothing like the International Column": Matthews, p. 207.

77   "there would someday be a world of people": Bessie, *Men in Battle*, p. 30.

77   "From the first day of the outbreak": Szurek, p. 83.

77   "We must know": Duberman, *Paul Robeson*, p. 220; "The artist must take sides," Robeson in Boyle and Bunie, *Paul Robeson*, p. 377. There are a number of easily available videos in which Robeson talks about the cause of Spain, including http://www.alba-valb.org/resources/robeson-primary-resources/paul-robeson-activism—speech.

78   "I've met wide-awake Negroes": Langston Hughes, "Negroes in Spain," The Volunteer for Liberty, 1937, available at http://www.english.illinois.edu/maps/poets/gl/hughes/inspain.htm.

78   "I cut pictures of women guerrillas out of the papers": Jackson, *British Women and the Spanish Civil War*, p. 192.

78   "an indifference to danger": Regler, *The Owl of Minerva*, p. 284.

79   "In Spain today": Shirsho Dasgupta, "Eighty Years Later: A Homage to Catalonia: Indians and the Spanish Civil War," *The Wire*, May 22, 2016.

79–80 "The flags of Great Britain": Bessie, *Men in Battle*, p. 45.

80   "Spain was the threatened friend": Regler, p. 271.

80   "quite different from anything that had gone before": Orwell, p. 101.

CHAPTER SIX

83   In September, *Vu* ran a huge spread: Vaill, p.57; Whelan, *This Is War!*, p. 66.

85   "The fascists were standing": Barea in Preston, *TSCW*, p. 88.

86   "loose brown Glengarry caps": George Esenwein, "Defence of Madrid," *The Spanish Civil War: A Modern Tragedy*, p. 57.

86   These volunteers are swiftly dispatched: Anderson, *The Spanish Civil War*, pp. 57–59.

86   "With eyes still wounded by sleep": Pablo Neruda, "Madrid (1936)," *Spain in Our Hearts*, p. 9.

88   "now it had a stripped appearance": Vaill, p. 83; Herbst, *The Starched Blue Sky of Spain*, pp. 136–137.

88–89 Here Capa meets Gustav Regler: The account of Capa's meeting with Regler and Lukács combines several sources, secondary and primary. We have also combined two Gustav Regler interviews with Josefa Stuart in which he retold the incident.

88   "in a halo of blue smoke": Lebrun and Lefebvre, p. 120.

88   "Maybe he'd like me to take him there on horseback": Lebrun and Lefebvre, p. 120.

90   "You've got me trapped by the Moors!": Regler, interview by Stuart, 1959, ICP.

90   "My intestines were not so brave as my camera": Regler, interview by Stuart, 1959, ICP.

90   "delicate scientific instruments": John Sommerfield, in Guttman, *The Wound in the Heart*, p. 87.

92   A proud capital: Wyden, p. 230.

94   "It is better to be the widow": Wyden, p. 196.

94   "side by side, arm in arm": Barea, *The Forging of a Rebel*, p. 601.

96   "insulted": Kershaw, p. 52.

CHAPTER SEVEN

99   "Capa changed photography": Gisèle Freund, interview by Richard Whelan, Dec. 18, 1981, ICP. For further information about photography, layout, design, and magazines in this period—and a great many examples—see chapters 26, 28, and 32 in Michel Frizot, ed., *A New History of Photography*; for examples of Capa's and Taro's images used in layouts as discussed in the text, see Frizot and de Veigy, *Vu*, and Lebrun and Lefebvre, *Robert Capa: The Paris Years*.

100 "automatic sense": Henri Cartier-Bresson, interview by Josefa Stuart, Feb. 6, 1959, ICP.

105 "What was new and prophetic": Martha Gellhorn, *The Face of War*, p. 22.

105 The first issue sells: Whelan, *This Is War!*, p. 48.

CHAPTER EIGHT

109 "a race against death": Cockburn, *Cockburn in Spain*, p. 148.

110 "seventy miles of people": T. C. Worsley in Preston, *TSCW*, p. 100.

114 "Of all the places to be in the world": Matthews, p. 185.

114 "He seemed to be able": Regler, interview by Stuart, 1959.

114–115 "Their faces glowed": Rogoyska, pp. 118–119.

116 She wears her long raincoat, a beret, sometimes stockings and heels: This description is derived from images retrieved in the Mexican Suitcase, where Taro in these clothes can be seen in the corner of one image with the Leica hanging by a strap around her neck (Young, *The Mexican Suitcase*, vol. 2, p. 156).

118 "Surrealism": Robert Capa and Gerda Taro, in notebook 7, Archives Nationales de France, digital version courtesy ICP.

118 "You could see people around Madrid": Martha Gellhorn, "High Explosive for Everyone" in *The Face of War*, p. 25.

119 "At the end of the avenue": Cowles in Adam Hochschild, *Spain in Our Hearts* (Boston: Houghton Mifflin Harcourt, 2016), p. 162.

CHAPTER NINE

122 "She was more realistic": Berg to Wyden, Mar. 27, 1987.

123 *copains*: This interpretation of the word *copain* comes from Irme Schaber, who illuminated its meaning as it was understood within Capa and Taro's political, artistic, and social circles, in *Gerda Taro: Fotoreporterin*, p. 149.

125 Just as she and Capa reinvented themselves: Schaber, *Gerda Taro: Fotoreporterin*, p. 149.

126 "great courage": Regler, interview by Stuart, 1959.

126 Even journalists: Matthews, p. 252.

126 "Madrid will be the tomb of fascism!": A. L. Strong in Esenwein, p. 56.

126 "The strafing from machine guns": Matthews, p. 263.

126 "nothing more to be seen": Matthews, p. 266.

127 "It was terrible": Vaill, p. 141.

CHAPTER TEN

133 "with a fringe of men": Barea, p. 655.

136 "I soon adopted him as a father": Capa, p. 129.

138 there are mistakes: Vernon, *Hemingway's Second War*, p. 29; Virginia Cowles, *Looking for Trouble*, p. 30.

139 "I turned round and saw some youths": Orwell, p. 121.

140 "The war and the revolution are inseparable": Orwell, p. 61.

140–141 "I used to sit on the roof": Orwell, p. 130.

142 "long French loaves, mounds of butter," Regler, p. 315.

142 Taro's family, back in Germany: Irme Schaber, "In the Picture with Irme Schaber: The Life and Work of Gerda Taro," lecture at Frontline Club, London, Oct. 17, 2008, frontlineclub.org.

CHAPTER ELEVEN

145 "very simple, moving photographs": Allen, prologue to Capa, *Death in the Making*.

147 "We found ourselves together": Allen, prologue.

147 "if your pictures aren't": Fred Ritchin, "Close Witness: The Involvement of the Photojournalist" in Frizot, *A New History of Photography*, p. 591.

148 "He was truly brave": Regler, interview by Stuart, ICP.

148 "incompatibility of being a reporter": Capa, p. 33.

150 "I want to make movies more than anything else": Capa, letter to Julia Friedman and his nieces, February 1935, ICP.

151 swollen to more than a million: Cowles, *Looking for Trouble*, p. 5.

151 "seemed to have nothing better to do": Cowles, p. 6.

152 bring movie flood lamps: Taro, telegram to Capa, May 18, 1937, ICP.

CHAPTER TWELVE

156 "a warm voice with a full timbre": Geza Korvin Karpathi interview, ICP.

156 "We all loved Gerda": Szurek, p. 171.

156 "I want to make movies": Robert Capa to Julia Friedmann and his neices, February 1935, ICP.

158 "You felt that you were taking part in a crusade": Hemingway, *For Whom the Bell Tolls*, p. 235.

159 "She was right alongside him in everything": Cartier-Bresson, interview by Stuart, Jan. 23, 1959.

160 "Better there than my heart": Schaber, p. 185; Vaill, p. 209.

160 "The Spanish Civil War was ideal for Capa": Regler, interview by Stuart, Feb. 27, 1959.

162 "Capa was an agreeable": Joris Ivens interview, ICP.

162 "the charming lady reporter": Irme Schaber, "Preliminary Remarks on Gerda Taro's Documentation of the Defense of the Andalusian Mining Region, Córdoba Front," in *The Mexican Suitcase*, ed. by Young, vol. 2, p. 241.

162 "You could hear the peals of female laughter": Kantorowicz in Rogoyska, p. 173.

163 "Never had I seen so many well-shaven men here": Rogoyska, p. 177.

163–164 "She confidently believed": Maspero, p. 56.

164 *La pequeña rubia*: Schaber, p. 185.

164 "Get out!": Orwell, p. 204.

164 "a peculiar evil feeling in the air": Orwell, p. 195.

164–165 they cannot go to their homes, which "had been raided": Orwell, p. 215.

165 "It is a terrible thing": Orwell, p. 219.

CHAPTER THIRTEEN

167 "spoiled children's party": Wyden, p. 394.

168 Taro and Capa are circling: The description of Taro at the writers' conference is abetted by a Soviet news film where we can glimpse her for a few seconds: Roman Karmen and Boris Makasseyev, *K Sobitiyam V Ispani*, July 1937. https://www.youtube.com/watch?v=HOFtmb2ds9Q. See 6:03–6:16. Our thanks to Amanda Vaill for bringing the film to our attention.

168 "wrapped in the tragic": Schaber, p. 223.

170 "I leave Gerda in your charge": Ted Allan, "Gerda," in *Ted Allan: A Partial Biography*, normanallan.com.

171–172 "There were more men": Matthews, p. 296.

172 By evening they had captured: Esenwein, *TSCW*, p. 217.

172–173 On their way back to Madrid: This description draws from Léon Moussinac, "Hommage à Gerda Taro," *Regards*, Aug. 5, 1937; Vaill, p. 220.

173 Gellhorn has a personal friendship: Moorehead, *Selected Letters of Martha Gellhorn*, pp. 55–56.

174 "with a mop on photographic paper": Lefebvre and Lebrun, "Where Does the Mexican Suitcase Come From?" p. 80.

176 "terrible battle under a burning July sun": Buckley, *The Life and Death of the Spanish Republic*, p. 326.

177 "in an alcove in a corner": Allen, prologue to Capa, *Death in the Making*.

178 "When one isn't in Madrid": Allen, prologue.

181 "guessed that Death danced with us": Freundlich, *The Traveling Years*, p. 53.

CHAPTER FOURTEEN

183 "The fascists brought their airplanes": Szurek, p. 158.

184 "We ran in advances": David McKelvy White in Hochschild, p. 228.

185 But in leading the charge against the rebels on Mosquito Ridge, Law is mortally wounded: See Appendix B.

185 "There, behind the dark, flashing cloud": Barea, pp. 681–682.

186 "We saw tough guys": David McKelvy White in Hochschild, p. 228.

187 "If we ever do get out of this": From *Ce Soir*, July 29, 1937, in Rogoyska, p. 212; Whelan, *Robert Capa: A Biography*, p. 122.

188 "really the only way": Marc Ribecourt, in Rogoyska, p. 225.

189–194 The account of Taro's last hours and death draws largely on Ted Allan's unpublished memoir, *Ted Allan: A Partial Biography*, at normanallan.com. Allan was the only person with Taro during the Brunete battle, and the single source for the dialogue comes from him. However, scholars have questioned Allan's account, since he was in love with Taro and believed they would leave for Canada together and get married. That was his wish, fantasy, or perhaps something concocted out of flirtatious hints she dropped. He did admit in later interviews that he did not always understand the dynamics between Capa and Taro. (See note on *copain*, text p. 123, note p. 278).While it is irresistible to use the dialogue he recorded, readers should treat it as an interested party's retrospective evocation of the moment, not a word-perfect transcript. We have tried to draw only the most essential moments from his description. The description of Taro at

the hospital derives from an account by the nurse, Irene Goldin Spiegel, interviewed by Irme Schaber in Vienna, Sept. 12, 2000, and another interview with her by Alex Kershaw.

189 "I must get some good pictures": Ted Allan, "Gerda," *Ted Allan: A Partial Biography*.

190 And so they push on: Allan, "Gerda."

190 "Of all the days to come!": Allan, "Gerda."

191 "fast, ugly arrow-heads": Hemingway, p. 87.

191 "Have you ever been under fire?": Allan, "Gerda."

191 "pictures of the dust": Allan, "Gerda."

192 "Tonight we'll have a farewell party": Rogoyska, p. 22; Allan, "Gerda."

194 "Did someone take care of my cameras?": Schaber, p. 209.

194 A French journalist, Mlle. Tarot: Vaill, p. 229.

CHAPTER FIFTEEN

197 Then the brother swings: Vaill, p. 230.

198 "I could not forget Gerda Taro": Rogoyska, p. 222.

198 One of her colleagues: Rogoyska, p. 225.

198 "He was just a great boy": Louis Aragon, in Vaill, p. 231.

198–200 "It was the middle of the day, and Capa was drunk," Regler, interview by Josefa Stuart, ICP, no date.

200 "I left her in danger": Pierre Gassmann, by Alex Kershaw, in

Blood and Champagne, p. 61.

201 "You learned the dry-mouthed": Hemingway, p. 236.

201 "It doesn't seem fair that I'm still alive": Cockburn in Allen, prologue to Capa, *Death in the Making*.

201 "Part of Capa died with Gerda": Kershaw, p. 62.

201 "When she died": Cartier-Bresson, interview by Stuart, Jan. 23, 1959.

CHAPTER SIXTEEN

202 "Comrades of the International": Ben Hughes, *They Shall Not Pass* (Oxford, England: Osprey Publishing, 2011), p. 212.

204 "His closest friends sensed another side of him": Whelan, *Robert Capa: A Biography*, p. 127.

204 "came and went as he chose": Gellhorn, "Death Do Us Part," in *The Trouble I've Seen*, p. 274.

204 "He made no plans, he roamed": Gellhorn, "Death Do Us Part," p. 282.

204 "How could you not": Vaill, p. 249.

205 "who spent one year at the Spanish front, and who stayed on": Robert Capa, dedication to *Death in the Making*.

206 "Here the moral[e] is bad": Robert Capa to Julia Fried-mann, 1938, ICP.

207 "one of the world's best news photographers": *Life* magazine in Whelan, *This Is War!*, pp. 156–157.

208 cold autumn night: Capa, translated by Whelan in *This Is*

War!, p.165; original notes for *Picture Post*, Dec. 3, 1938.

209 "The Greatest War-Photographer in the World: Robert Capa": *Picture Post*, Dec. 3, 1938.

209 "Life's Camera Gets Closer": *Life*, Dec. 12, 1938.

210 "Words are hardly necessary": Capa, translated by Whelan in *This Is War!*, p. 172; original notes for *Picture Post*, Dec. 3, 1938.

210 "the enemy increases its artillery fire": Capa, translated by Whelan in *This Is War!*, p. 181; original notes for *Picture Post*, Dec. 3, 1938.

211 "I want to die": In *Match*, Dec. 12, 1938; in Whelan, *This Is War!*, p. 155.

211 "I was so sick": Robert Capa to Julia Friedmann, Dec. 10, 1937, in Whelan, *Robert Capa: A Biography*, p. 156.

212 "It is not easy": Robert Capa, *This Is War!*, p. 195.

212–213 "Each bomber had four to eight machine guns": Whelan, *This Is War!*, p. 186.

213   "is the gamble shared by all of the refugees": Whelan, *This Is War!*, pp. 191–193.

213   "Hundreds and hundreds of thousands": Whelan, *This Is War!*, p. 197.

214–215 She tells of flower sellers in Barcelona: Gellhorn, *The Face of War*, p. 41.

216   Chim's assignment was a ticket to safety: Young, *The Mexican Suitcase*, Vol. 1, p. 95.

217   Knowing he would be targeted: Young, *The Mexican Suitcase*, Vol. 1, p. 95.

CHAPTER SEVENTEEN

219   "greatest amphibious": General Eisenhower in Kershaw, p. 121.

221   "the most important story of the century": Kershaw, p. 126. Capa's ruined and blurry photos are so iconic that they form the basis for the opening of Steven Spielberg's film *Saving Private Ryan*—a long opening sequence of the invasion that draws specifically from Capa's images.

221   "I felt . . . that the whole world was waiting": Whelan, *Robert Capa: A Biography*, p. 214.

222   "Rush, rush, rush!": Kershaw, p. 129.

224   "Why be exploited by others?": Kershaw, p. 179.

228–229 "It's not a job for a grown man": Whelan, *Robert Capa: A Biography*, p. 293.

229   "I can't be forty, how can anybody be forty?": Kershaw, p. 239.

230   On May 25, 1954: Kershaw, p. 246.

230–231 "I'm going up the road a little bit": Whelan, *Robert Capa: A Biography*, p. 299.

231   "I realize now": Julia Friedmann interview, ICP.

CHAPTER EIGHTEEN

235   it was as if Taro became part of Capa: Schaber, Frontline Club lecture, Oct. 17, 2008.

CHAPTER NINETEEN

239   "Two disparate pieces of a jigsaw puzzle": Brian Wallis, Tricia Ziff, *The Mexican Suitcase*, film.

240   "Curiously enough": Orwell, p. 230.

240   "We lived those years intensely": Lisa Berger and Carol Mazer, directors, *De toda la vida* [All our lives], 1986.

240   "Youth was born in Spain": Allen, prologue to Capa, *Death in the Making*.

240   In Poland alone: Naggar, *Chim: Children of War*, p. 8.

241   "We shall be one person": Steichen, *The Family of Man*, photo caption.

242   his "first fascist corpse": Szurek, p. 93.

242   "was just as much against oppression of the Left": Cornell Capa, interview and notes, ICP, no date.

BIBLIOGRAPHY

19 de Julio en Nueva York: un año de lucha y de trabajo. New York: s.n., 1937.

Alpert, Michael. *A New International History of the Spanish Civil War.* New York: Palgrave Macmillan, 2004.

Anderson, James M. *The Spanish Civil War: A History and Reference Guide.* Westport: Greenwood Press, 2003.

Andrés, Sanz, Jesús de. Atlas ilustrado de *carteles de la guerra civil española.* Madrid: Susaeta, 2010.

Balfour, Sebastian. *The End of the Spanish Empire: 1898–1923.* Oxford: Clarendon Press, 1997.

Barea, Arturo. *The Forging of a Rebel.* Translated by Ilsa Barea. New York: Viking Press, 1972.

Bessie, Alvah Cecil. *Alvah Bessie's Spanish Civil War Notebooks.* Edited by Dan Bessie. Lexington: University Press of Kentucky, 2002.

———. *Men in Battle: A Story of Americans in Spain.* San Francisco: Chandler & Sharp, 1975. First published in 1939 by Scribner.

Blinkhorn, Martin, ed. *Spain in Conflict 1931–1939: Democracy and Its Enemies.* London: Sage Publications, 1986.

Boyle, Sheila Tully, and Andrew Bunie. *Paul Robeson: The Years of Promise and Achievement.* Amherst: University of Massachusetts Press, 2001.

Browder, Earl, and Bill Lawrence. *Next Steps to Win the War in Spain.* New York: Workers Library, 1938.

Buckley, Henry. *The Life and Death of the Spanish Republic: A Witness to the Spanish Civil War.* New York: I.B. Tauris, 2013.

Capa, Robert. *Slightly Out of Focus.* New York: Random House, 1999.

Carulla, Jordi, and Arnau Carulla. *The Color of War: Spanish Civil War 1936–1939.* Barcelona: Postermil, 2000.

Casanova, Julián. *The Spanish Republic and Civil War.* Translated by Martin Douch. Cambridge: Cambridge University Press, 2010.

Cockburn, Claud. *Cockburn in Spain: Despatches from the Spanish Civil War.* Edited by James Pettifer. London: Lawrence and Wishart, 1986.

Collum, Danny Duncan, ed., and Victor A. Berch. *African Americans in the Spanish Civil War: "This Ain't Ethiopia, But It'll Do."* New York: G.K. Hall, 1992.

Defence of Madrid. Directed by Ivor Montagu. United Kingdom: Progressive Film Institute, 1936.

Dos Passos, John. *Adventures of a Young Man.* New York: Harcourt Brace, 1939.

———. *Century's Ebb: The Thirteenth Chronicle.* Boston: Gambit, 1975.

———. *Travel Books and Other Writings 1916–1941.* New York: Library of America, 2003.

Duberman, Martin Bauml. *Paul Robeson.* New York: Knopf, 1988.

Escolar, Hipólito. *La cultura durante la guerra civil.* Madrid: Alhambra, 1987.

Esenwein, George R. *The Spanish Civil War: A Modern Tragedy.* New York: Taylor & Francis, 2005.

Freundlich, Elisabeth. *The Traveling Years.* Translated by Elizabeth Pennebaker. Riverside, CA: Ariadne Press, 1999.

Frizot, Michel, and Cédric de Veigy. *Vu: The Story of a Magazine That Made an Era.* Translated by Ruth Sharman. London: Thames & Hudson, 2009.

Gellhorn, Martha. *The Trouble I've Seen.* New York: William Morrow, 1936.

———. *The View from the Ground.* New York: Atlantic Monthly, 1988.

Glazer, Peter. *Radical Nostalgia*: Spanish Civil War Commemoration in America. Rochester, NY: University of Rochester Press, 2005.

Guerra de la Vega, Ramón. *La guerra civil: España 1936–1939.* Pozuelo de Alarcón, Spain: Guerra de la Vega, 1996.

Guttmann, Allen. *The Wound in the Heart: America and the Spanish Civil War.* New York: Free Press of Glencoe, 1962.

Hardt, Hanno. "Remembering Capa, Spain, and the Legacy of Gerda Taro, 1936–1937." *On Photography, History, and Memory in Spain*. Edited by Maria Nilsson. *Hispanic Issues On Line Debates* 3 (Spring 2011): 30–38.

Hart, Stephen M., ed. *"¡No Pasarán!" Art, Literature, and the Spanish Civil War*. London: Tamesis, 1988.

Hemingway, Ernest. *The Fifth Column*. New York: Scribner, 1938.

————. *For Whom the Bell Tolls*. New York: Scribner, 1940.

Herbst, Josephine. *The Starched Blue Sky of Spain and Other Memoirs*. Boston: Northeastern University Press, 1999.

Hochschild, Adam. *Spain in Our Hearts: Americans in the Spanish Civil War, 1936–1939*. New York: Houghton Mifflin Harcourt, 2016.

Hughes, Ben. *They Shall Not Pass! The British Battalion at Jarama—The Spanish Civil War*. Oxford, England: Osprey Publishing, 2011.

Jackson, Angela. *British Women and the Spanish Civil War*. Barcelona: Warren & Pell, 2009.

Keene, Judith. *Fighting for Franco: International Volunteers in Nationalist Spain During the Spanish Civil War, 1936–1939*. London: Leicester University Press, 2001.

Kershaw, Alex. *Blood and Champagne: The Life and Times of Robert Capa*. Cambridge, MA: Da Capo Press, 2004.

Kuromiya, Hiroaki. *Stalin: Profiles in Power*. Harlow: Pearson Education, 2005.

Langer, Elinor. *Josephine Herbst: The Story She Could Never Tell*. Boston: Atlantic Monthly, 1984.

Lebrun, Bernard, and Michel Lefebvre. *Robert Capa: The Paris Years, 1933–1954*. New York: Abrams, 2012.

Lines, Lisa Margaret. *Milicianas: Women in Combat in the Spanish Civil War*. Lanham, MD: Lexington Books, 2012.

Ludington, Townsend. *John Dos Passos: A Twentieth-Century Odyssey*. New York: Carroll & Graf, 1998.

MacDougall, Ian, ed. *Voices from the Spanish Civil War: Personal Recollections of Scottish Volunteers in Republican Spain*. Edinburgh: Polygon, 1986.

Maspero, François. *Out of the Shadows: A Life of Gerda Taro*. Translated by Geoffrey Strachan. London: Souvenir Press, 2008.

Matthews, Herbert L. *Two Wars and More to Come*. New York: Carrick & Evans, 1938.

Mazower, Mark. *Dark Continent: Europe's Twentieth Century*. New York: Knopf, 1998.

McLoughlin, Kate. *Martha Gellhorn: The War Writer in the Field and in the Text*. Manchester: Manchester University Press, 2007.

Mendelson, Jordana. *The Spanish Pavilion Paris, 1937*. Barcelona: Ediciones de La Central, 2009.

Miller, Russell. *Magnum: Fifty Years at the Front Line of History*. New York: Grove Press, 1997.

Moorehead, Caroline. *Gellhorn: A Twentieth-Century Life*. New York: Henry Holt, 2003.

————, ed. *Selected Letters of Martha Gellhorn*. New York: Henry Holt, 2006.

Morris, John G. *Get the Picture: A Personal History of Photojournalism*. Chicago: University of Chicago Press, 2002.

Naggar, Carole. *Chim: Children of War*. Brooklyn: Umbrage Editions, 2013.

Neruda, Pablo. *Spain in Our Hearts: Hymn to the Glories of the People at War*. Translated by Donald D. Walsh. New York: New Directions, 2005.

Orwell, George. *Homage to Catalonia*. New York: Harcourt Brace, 1952.

Payne, Stanley G. *The Collapse of the Spanish Republic, 1933–1936*. New Haven, CT: Yale University Press, 2006.

————. *Fascism in Spain, 1923–1977*. Madison: University of Wisconsin Press, 1999.

————. *The Spanish Civil War, the Soviet Union, and Communism*. New Haven, CT: Yale University Press, 2004.

Pemán, José María. *Comentarios a mil imágenes de la guerra civil española*. Barcelona: Editorial AHR, 1967.

Preston, Paul, ed. *Revolution and War in Spain: 1931–1939*. London: Methuen, 1984.

————. *The Spanish Civil War, 1936–1939*. London: Weidenfeld and Nicolson, 1986.

Regler, Gustav. *The Owl of Minerva: The Autobiography of Gustav Regler*. Translated by Norman Denny. New York: Farrar, Straus & Cudahy, 1969.

Rhodes, Richard. *Hell and Good Company: The Spanish Civil War and the World It Made*. New York: Simon & Schuster, 2015.

Robles, Tardío, Rocío. *Art and Civil War*. Barcelona: Ediciones de La Central, 2010.

Rogoyska, Jane. *Gerda Taro: Inventing Robert Capa*. London: Jonathan Cape, 2013.

Rollyson, Carl. *Nothing Ever Happens to the Brave: The Story of Martha Gellhorn*. New York: St. Martin's Press, 1990.

Salvador, Tomás. *Guerra de españa en sus fotografías*. Barcelona: Ediciones Marte, 1966.

Schaber, Irme. *Gerda Taro: Fotoreporterin; Mit Robert Capa in Spanishen Bürgerkrieg*. Stuttgart, Germany: Jonas Verlag, 2013.

Schaber, Irme, Richard Whelan, and Kristen Lubben, eds. *Gerda Taro*. New York: International Center of Photography, 2007.

Schlögel, Karl. *Moscow, 1937*. Translated by Rodney Livingstone. Cambridge, UK: Polity, 2012.

Snyder, Timothy. *Bloodlands: Europe Between Hitler and Stalin*. New York: Basic, 2010.

Solé i Sabaté, Josep M., and Joan Villarroya. *Guerra i propaganda: fotografies del comissariat de propaganda de la generalitat de Catalunya (1936–1939)*. Barcelona: Arxiu Nacional de Catalunya, 2006.

Steichen, Edward. *The Family of Man*. New York: Museum of Modern Art, 1986.

Szurek, Aleksander. *The Shattered Dream*. Translated by Jacques Grunblatt and Hilda Grunblatt. Boulder, CO: East European Monographs, 1989.

Thomas, Hugh. *The Spanish Civil War*. New York: Harper & Row, 1977.

Tismaneanu, Vladimir. *The Devil in History: Communism, Fascism, and Some Lessons of the Twentieth Century*. Berkeley: University of California Press, 2012.

Vaill, Amanda. *Hotel Florida: Truth, Love, and Death in the Spanish Civil War*. New York: Farrar, Straus and Giroux, 2014.

Vernon, Alex. *Hemingway's Second War: Bearing Witness to the Spanish Civil War*. Iowa City: University of Iowa Press, 2011.

Whelan, Richard. *Robert Capa: A Biography*. Lincoln: University of Nebraska Press, 1985.

———. *Robert Capa: Photographs*. New York: Aperture, 1996.

———. *This Is War! Robert Capa at Work*. New York: International Center of Photography/Steidl, 2007.

Wyden, Peter. *The Passionate War: The Narrative History of the Spanish Civil War*. New York: Simon & Schuster, 1983.

Yates, James. *Mississippi Mud: Memoir of a Black American in the Abraham Lincoln Brigade*. Seattle: Open Hand Publishing, 1989.

Young, Cynthia, ed. *The Mexican Suitcase: The Rediscovered Spanish Civil War Negatives of Capa, Chim, and Tara*. 2 vols. New York: International Center of Photography, 2010.

———, ed. *We Went Back: Photographs from Europe 1933–1956 by Chim*. New York: International Center of Photography, 2013.

WEB RESOURCES

The Eyes of the World deals with many people, ideas, artistic creations, and events that can be explored on the Web. Here we offer an initial introduction to some sites we found to be particularly rich, interesting, and useful.

SPANISH CIVIL WAR

The first and best central digital spot for the Spanish Civil War is the Trabajadores site at the University of Warwick in England: www2.warwick.ac.uk/go/scw. Not only does it provide digital access to the university's rich collection of civil war materials from the point of view of left-wing and communist English unions, but on its Find Out More tab, it presents a detailed time line of the war and a spectacular collection of international links in many media.

A site on the International Brigades from all nations, with many colorful posters: internationalbrigadesinspain.weebly.com.

For the American side of the story of the International Brigades, the Abraham Lincoln Brigade Archives are an excellent resource: alba-valb.org. ALBA has a distinct point of view—honoring and supporting those who served the cause of the Spanish Republic. Keeping that perspective in mind, the site is well organized, easy to use, and includes video as well as images and text on its Education page.

Henri Cartier-Bresson's short film "With the Abraham Lincoln Brigade in Spain" has a possible link to Capa. It is available on YouTube.

For teachers who would like to use Paul Robeson in a unit, here is a lesson plan with resources: www.archives.gov/education/lessons/robeson.

A couple of highlights from the rich digital resources of Spanish Civil War materials at the Mandeville Special Collections Library at University of California at San Diego: They Still Draw Pictures, drawings by children recording the conflict: http://libraries.ucsd.edu/speccoll/tsdp.

Adhesive Propaganda: Stamps of the Spanish Civil War: http://libraries.ucsd.edu/speccoll/swstamps/#russian.

ROBERT CAPA, GERDA TARO

For both of their photos, begin here: magnumphotos.com and icp.org.

You can listen to a rare radio interview with Capa from 1947 on YouTube and hear the only recording of his voice while looking at some of his images.

Also available on YouTube is a full-length PBS biography of Capa from 2003, American Masters' *Robert Capa: In Love and War.*

The March of Time newsreel "Rehearsal for War" contains a bit of footage of loyalist soldiers in Spain filmed by Capa (it's a very small image and will not play on Chrome browser): http://xroads.virginia.edu/~ma04/wood/mot/html/spain.htm.

You can glimpse the golden-haired Taro for about ten seconds in a 1937 Soviet documentary, *K sobitiyam v ispanii No 20,* available on YouTube. See the 6:03 mark.

OTHER PHOTOGRAPHERS CLOSELY LINKED TO CAPA AND TARO

For Chim's photos, begin here: davidseymour.com.

For Henri Cartier-Bresson's photos, begin at Magnum as well: magnumphotos.com.

For Fred Stein's photos, begin here: fredstein.com.

For André Kertész's photos, begin here: http://www.atgetphotography.com/The-Photographers/Andre-Kertesz.html.

TO VIEW GUERNICA

Online: http://www.museoreinasofia.es/en/collection/artwork/guernica.

The painting is held at the Reina Sofia Museum in Madrid and is well worth seeing in person. In addition to *Guernica,* the museum hosts a permanent exhibit on the art shown in the 1937 pavilion: http://www.museoreinasofia.es/sites/default/files/salas/informacion/206_06_eng_pabellon_esp-goya-guernica.pdf.

1937 SPANISH PAVILION

A replica of the pavilion was built in Barcelona in 1992, and you can see it here: http://www.spainisculture.com/en/monumentos/barcelona/pabellon_de_espana_en_la_exposicion_internacional_de_paris_de_1937.html.

For more information about the pavilion and *Guernica,* visit PBS's Treasures of the World site: http://www.pbs.org/treasuresoftheworld.

GARCÍA LORCA VIDEOS

A musical performance of "Romance Sonambulo" by Spanish singers Ana Belén and Manzanita can be seen on YouTube.

Hear a recitation of "At five in the afternoon" lines from García Lorca's "Lament for Ignacio Sánchez Mejías" in a clip from a 1997 fictional movie based on his death also on YouTube.